Cryptocurrency Uncovered

Your Guide Through the Digital Gold Rush

by

Nathan Venture. D

NATHAN

To You,

Thank you!

Table of Contents

Introduction: Navigating the Digital Gold Rush

The digital age has ushered in a revolution that extends far beyond our smartphones and social media profiles. It's shaken the very foundations of financial transactions and shifted our concept of money into a domain that's both exhilarating and, at times, baffling. We've entered a new era of digital currencies—where computer codes and decentralized networks are just as valuable, if not more so, than traditional banknotes. This is the digital gold rush, and understanding its rules, players, and potential rewards is crucial for anyone looking to participate.

Amid this burgeoning digital economy, cryptocurrencies and blockchain technology have emerged as groundbreaking innovations. They present a transformative economic force that carries the potential to redefine commerce, banking, and the flow of capital worldwide. Approaching these technologies can be daunting. Yet, with the right guidance, anyone can unlock their complexities and navigate this new terrain with confidence.

This book serves as your compass through the ever-evolving landscape of cryptocurrencies. Its pages offer clarity on blockchain technology's fundamentals and a focused exploration of how digital currencies like Bitcoin and numerous altcoins are reshaping the concept of wealth. We delve deep without assuming pre-existing expertise, ensuring beginners and those with a foundational understanding can both find value in the lessons shared.

We begin by charting the course that has led to the rise of digital currency. It's a tale of innovation, disruption, and the relentless pursuit of a more inclusive and decentralized financial system. As we recount the birth of this new era, you'll gain insights into the technological marvels and strategic boldness that have propelled cryptocurrencies from a niche hobby to a significant global phenomenon.

The core of this digital revolution is blockchain technology. A marvel of modern computer science, blockchain has extended its reach well beyond mere financial transactions. We explain in clear terms what blockchain is, how it works, and why it's considered one of this century's most significant innovations. Understanding the mechanisms that secure and validate cryptocurrency transactions is key to appreciating their potential and resilience.

Moving from technology to practice, we present the integral steps for investing in cryptocurrencies. First-time buyers, don't be intimidated—this book provides the required foundation to set up your digital wallet, navigate exchanges, and complete your initial transactions with confidence. Experienced investors will find advanced strategies for risk management and portfolio diversification to enhance their decision-making processes.

Mining for cryptocurrencies is akin to prospecting for gold. It's a competitive and complex process that involves powerful hardware, sophisticated algorithms, and a network of peers. We break down how mining works and how to select appropriate hardware, ensuring that readers interested in this space have the knowledge they need to get started.

However, success in the digital gold rush is not merely about getting your hands on cryptocurrencies. It's also about understanding and navigating the intricate web of regulations that govern their use. From anti-money laundering (AML) policies to global legal frameworks, we explain the regulatory landscape, helping you remain compliant and informed.

With the allure of these digital assets comes the necessity of safeguarding them. Recognizing risks, protecting investments, and understanding the role of cryptography and cybersecurity are paramount. Our discussions on security practices will equip you with the tools to defend your digital treasure.

As we transition from present realities to consider future possibilities, we contemplate cryptocurrency's place within the broader context of global finance. What role will digital currencies play in the evolution of payment systems and the global economy? How should one prepare for a decentralized future? These are critical questions that we address, painting a picture of what lies ahead on the horizon of this digital revolution.

We also acknowledge the engineers and innovators who build upon blockchain technologies—those who push the boundaries of what's possible. Learning about the developers' landscape and how blockchain projects transition from concept to execution will inspire current and future creators to leave their mark on this digital frontier.

Blockchain's potential stretches beyond just currency; it's a tool that can revolutionize industries from supply chain management to healthcare and real estate. We explore these alternative applications, shedding light on how the technology can offer solutions to age-old problems and inefficiencies.

In preparation for the next wave of innovation, it's imperative to stay informed about emerging technologies within the cryptospace. Our exploration of decentralized finance (DeFi), non-fungible tokens (NFTs), and other burgeoning trends will leave you enlightened and excited about the creative and economic possibilities that lay ahead.

As your guide through the digital gold rush, this book is more than just an introduction to cryptocurrency and blockchain. It's a comprehensive map and toolbox, designed to educate, inspire, and empower you as you navigate this transformative space. Let this be the beginning of your journey to financial sovereignty and technological fluency in a world where digital gold gleams with untapped potential.

Chapter 1: The Birth of Digital Currency

In an era where technological marvels unfold with each passing day, the birth of digital currency stands as a pivotal movement in the financial narrative of our times. Digital currency, the ingenious combination of cryptography and monetary theory, has redefined what we consider as 'money.' From its intriguing inception via the enigmatic paper by Satoshi Nakamoto, outlining the potential of a decentralized currency called Bitcoin, to its turbulent ascension amidst global economies, digital currency has carved a place in the market that's impossible to ignore. This chapter lays the foundation, allowing readers to grasp the magnitude of the shift from physical coins and paper notes to digital bits and blockchain ledgers. As we progress, keep in mind that what was once thought impossible is now a reality that's reshaping industries, empowering individuals, and challenging our very understanding of economic sovereignty.

Understanding Cryptocurrency

Embarking on the journey known as cryptocurrency can be exhilarating yet daunting. At its core, cryptocurrency is a form of digital or virtual currency that uses cryptography for security, making it difficult to counterfeit. Its decentralized nature - typically free from central authority intervention - distinguishes it from traditional fiat currencies and introduces a paradigm shift in how we perceive and interact with money.

Cryptocurrencies operate on a technology called blockchain, which is a distributed ledger enforced by a disparate network of computers. This innovative approach to recording transactions and managing assets has the potential to disrupt numerous industries. However, the focus within these pages remains on understanding cryptocurrencies as a digital asset class.

To grasp the essence of cryptocurrency, one must first appreciate the concept of digital ownership. Traditional banking systems keep track of money transfers via private ledgers accessible only by the banking institution. Conversely, cryptocurrency transactions are recorded on public ledgers, ensuring transparency while protecting users' anonymity through pseudonyms.

At the heart of cryptocurrency is the principle of decentralization. Unlike centralized banking systems, cryptocurrencies are typically maintained by a network of participants known as nodes, each holding a copy of the entire ledger. Decentralization eliminates the possibility of a single point of failure and distributes trust among participants.

Consider Bitcoin, the inaugural cryptocurrency, which laid the framework for subsequent digital currencies. It introduced a peer-to-peer electronic cash system where transactions don't require intermediaries. This model empowers users to transact directly with each other, thereby reducing fees and time delays that are characteristic of traditional financial transactions.

Still, one might wonder about the intrinsic value of these digital tokens. Cryptocurrencies derive their value from a combination of scarcity, utility, demand, and the security of their underlying blockchain. Tokens like Bitcoin have a capped supply, mimicking resources like gold, imbuing them with a deflationary character. Their utility is multifaceted, serving not just as money but as tokens that can represent access to services, rights within a system, or as a stake in a collective venture.

The question of legitimacy often arises with cryptocurrencies. Initially viewed with skepticism due to their association with illicit activities and speculation, cryptocurrencies are gaining legitimacy as institutions begin to explore their potential. Their digital nature and borderless transactions make them an attractive proposition for global commerce.

For those new to cryptocurrencies, understanding market dynamics is crucial. Volatility is a hallmark of cryptocurrency markets, often driven by sentiment, technological advancements, regulatory news, and market manipulation. Seasoned investors know that these fluctuations can be both an opportunity and a detriment, demanding a disciplined approach to investment.

As you consider immersing yourself in the cryptosphere, remember that diversification can mitigate risk. Just like traditional investments, not all cryptocurrencies are created equal. Each token comes with a unique set of features, use cases, and backing community strength. Analysis and due diligence are the cornerstones for navigating these digital waters smartly.

Understanding cryptocurrency also means getting to grips with wallets and exchanges. A digital wallet is where you store your cryptocurrency, while exchanges are platforms where you can buy, sell, or trade them. Each comes with its own security considerations, user interfaces, and support for different currencies.

It's impossible to discuss cryptocurrency without addressing mining. This is how transactions are processed and new coins created in some cryptocurrencies. Mining involves solving complex mathematical problems to validate transactions. It's a competitive and resource-intensive process that also serves to secure the network.

Furthermore, innovations within the cryptocurrency space are constantly evolving. Initial Coin Offerings (ICOs), Security Token

Offerings (STOs), and Non-Fungible Tokens (NFTs) are reshaping concepts of fundraising, asset ownership, and creative rights. They represent the bleeding edge of how blockchain and cryptographic principles can be applied.

Lastly, we cannot overlook the global regulatory response to cryptocurrencies. As governments worldwide begin to understand and adapt to this phenomenon, regulations are evolving. While some countries embrace the innovation cryptocurrency brings, others scrutinize it heavily, affecting market dynamics significantly.

As you continue on this journey, remember that cryptocurrency isn't just a technological phenomenon but a cultural and financial revolution as well. Its complexity may be overwhelming at first, but with patience and persistence, anyone can develop a firm understanding and potentially leverage its advantages. Navigate these digital waters thoughtfully, arm yourself with knowledge, and you will be well on your way to participating in this exciting new landscape.

History and Revolution of Money

The evolution of money is a spectacular narrative of innovation, societal shift, and technological ingenuity. At its core, money is a mechanism for facilitating trade, transcending the inefficiencies of barter systems. Over millennia, societies have witnessed the transition from primitive forms of money such as shells and beads to the precious metal coins of ancient empires.

The concept of coinage, first materializing in the kingdoms of Lydia and Ionia in the 7th century BCE, redefined trade, as did the later establishment of minted currency across various civilizations. The tangible value of these coins lay in their metal content, typically gold or silver, which established a standard for wealth and enabled more complex economic systems to flourish.

History pivoted again with the introduction of paper money during China's Tang dynasty. This innovation brought significant convenience but also necessitated a robust level of trust in the issuing authorities — a trust that they would redeem paper notes for tangible assets upon request. This evolution marked the early stages of fiat money, currency that holds value largely through governmental decree rather than intrinsic worth.

Moving forward to the Renaissance, the formation of banking institutions and the subsequent conceptualization of banknotes and credit further transformed the exchange medium. This shift saw the representation of money becoming increasingly abstract, physical tokens giving way to numbers in a ledger, yet the economic activity they stirred was anything but hypothetical.

The industrial era introduced checks and other non-cash instruments, seeding the beginning of digital transactions. The ethos driving these advancements centered on efficiency and security, always aiming to streamline commerce and preserve the user's wealth.

By the 20th century, centralized banking systems had become entrenched, with institutions like the Federal Reserve in the United States stabilizing and controlling national currencies. The Bretton Woods Agreement and the gold standard dictated international monetary policy, but by the 1970's, even this link to physical assets was mostly abandoned, reinforcing the fiat nature of modern currency.

Credit cards, introduced in the mid-20th century, and later online banking platforms in the 1990s, are milestones in the ongoing journey of money. These tools further distanced the conceptualization of money from physical objects, embedding financial movement into the digital realm.

However, the digital revolution truly came to a head with the explosion of the internet, which presented a fertile ground for yet another transformation. This rapidly expanding digital landscape paved the path for cryptocurrencies, where Bitcoin took the lead in 2009. Cryptocurrencies offer a digital ledger, or blockchain, which operates without the need for a central authority, making it a global and decentralized form of currency.

Bitcoin, and the many cryptocurrencies that followed, revolutionized not just our conception of what money could be but also challenged the frameworks upon which modern financial institutions are built. These digital assets have introduced a level of autonomy and anonymity previously unthinkable in the realm of finance.

Crucially, cryptocurrencies spotlight the potent potential of blockchain technology. This innovative ledger system establishes security and integrity in transactions without intermediaries. The cryptographic underpinnings also provide a safeguard against duplication and fraud, which is a significant leap forward compared to the paper and metal-based money of the past.

The journey from trade by barter to a world contemplating the implications of a digital currency that operates beyond borders and regulatory frameworks is a testament to human ingenuity. Each phase of money's evolution has been a response to the contemporaneous needs and capabilities of the times. Just as the transition to paper money required an immense cultural shift in trust, so too does the adoption of digital currencies challenge existing norms and provoke us to think differently about value exchange.

Crypto assets are also stirring global conversations about financial inclusion. By potentially removing the barriers that traditional banking systems erect, they propose a means by which to bring financial services to the unbanked or underbanked populations of the world. This inclusive promise is one of many reasons why the discourse around cryptocurrencies continues to gather momentum.

The revolution of money, from its tangible origins to its eminent digital future, illustrates our economic history and our aspiration to create an accessible, efficient, and equitable financial system. Whether or not cryptocurrencies will be the ultimate iteration of this system remains to be seen, but they are undoubtedly a significant milestone in the storied history of money.

Understanding this rich history isn't just an academic exercise; it provides context for why digital currencies have the potential to be more than just another asset class. They represent the natural progression of an ever-evolving quest to better service the economic needs and dynamics of societies across the globe.

While skeptics may question the sustainability and practicality of cryptocurrencies, believers and participants in the digital currency ecosystem recognize that much like every revolutionary form of money before, adaptation and widespread acceptance take time and patience. The revolution may not happen overnight, but the groundwork has been laid for a shift in our understanding and utilization of money that could redefine wealth, commerce, and the very fabric of economic interaction.

Key Players: From Satoshi Nakamoto to Mainstream Markets

In the pervasive journey of cryptocurrency from the fringes to the forefront of finance, a cadre of significant figures and institutions have played pivotal roles. In the incipient stages of this narrative, one mysterious figure looms large: Satoshi Nakamoto. The pseudonymous entity who authored the Bitcoin whitepaper and developed its first reference implementation paved the way for a decentralized digital currency revolution. Yet, the true identity of Nakamoto remains an enigma, with rampant speculation regarding who—or what—this trailblazer might be, serving as a catalyst for the ethos of decentralization that underscores the cryptocurrency ethos.

The release of Bitcoin triggered a cascade of innovation and ignited interest within a tightknit community primarily composed of cryptographers and software developers. These early adopters not only improved upon the protocol but also evangelized the concept of digital currencies. Among them, figures such as Hal Finney, the first recipient of a bitcoin transaction, remind one of the inherent altruism and curiosity driving this nascent technology's expansion.

Turning from individuals to entities, exchanges have been instrumental in catalyzing the transition of cryptocurrencies from theoretical constructs to tradable assets. Platforms like Mt. Gox, which later infamously collapsed, initially provided the liquidity necessary for Bitcoin's monetization. This pattern of growth and setback is not an anomaly but rather a consistent theme in the cryptocurrency saga, where resilience has proved as critical as innovation to sustainability.

Moreover, mainstream finance's embrace of cryptocurrency has been cautiously incremental. Institutions like Goldman Sachs and JPMorgan Chase, once sceptical of digital currencies, have pivoted to explore their potential. Their involvement signals a legitimization of the asset class, and their influence is facilitating broader market adoption amongst both retail and institutional investors.

Aside from financial institutions, technology corporations have also entered the crypto arena. Entities ranging from Microsoft to Overstock began accepting Bitcoin relatively early on, setting a precedent for commercial acceptance. The involvement of high-tech companies such as IBM and Intel in blockchain has further bolstered the underlying technology, pointing towards a future where crypto-currencies and blockchain are seamlessly integrated into everyday business operations.

In parallel to corporate players, government entities have played a more ambiguous role. While regulatory uncertainty has often hamstrung the development of crypto markets, some regions, like

Malta and Switzerland, have adopted a more welcoming stance, becoming hubs for blockchain enterprises. These countries are crafting a blueprint that others might follow, demonstrating that progressive regulatory frameworks can potentially foster innovation rather than stifle it.

Cryptocurrency's journey to mainstream markets has also been greatly influenced by thought leaders and influencers. Figures like Andreas M. Antonopoulos and Vitalik Buterin have provided education and guidance, contributing to a better understanding and acceptance of these technologies. Their speeches, books, and social media presence have been instrumental in shaping public opinion and drawing new enthusiasts into the crypto community.

It would be remiss not to mention the advent of Initial Coin Offerings (ICOs), which introduced a new avenue for projects to raise capital and for individuals to invest in early-stage blockchain ventures. This phenomenon has brought forth a fresh cast of players – startups and founders who, by leveraging blockchain technology, are redefining entrepreneurship and investment in the digital age.

Furthermore, the proliferation of digital asset custodial services has played a vital role in fostering institutional investment. Companies like Coinbase and Gemini provide the security and insurance mechanisms demanded by large investors, thereby acting as gateways for substantial capital flows into the cryptocurrency market.

Another pivotal development has been the rise of decentralized finance, or DeFi. This sector embodies the principle of disintermediation foundational to cryptocurrency's ethos and its key players – from lending protocols like Aave to decentralized exchanges such as Uniswap – are redefining notions of borrowing, lending, and trading. This represents an emerging domain where traditional financial structures are being challenged and reimagined.

Payment processors have also been instrumental in the propagation of cryptocurrency usage. Companies such as PayPal and Square have begun integrating cryptocurrencies into their platforms, allowing for easier acquisition, disposal, and use of digital assets by the mainstream public. Their involvement marks a significant milestone in bridging the gap between traditional finance and the realm of cryptocurrency.

Lastly, we turn to the enigmatic yet increasingly prevalent area of non-fungible tokens (NFTs). Artists, creators, and collectors have converged in this new market, which substantiates the ownership and uniqueness of digital assets in a way previously impossible. This intersection of technology, art, and commerce has made blockchain tangible to the wider public, providing a humanizing dimension to digital asset transactions.

In understanding the diverse array of entities and individuals who have contributed to the growth and mainstreaming of cryptocurrencies, one grasps the panoramic nature of this sphere. This evolution has been neither linear nor predictable, and future chapters will likely be written by an as-yet-unknown cast of visionaries and institutions. As they carve out their niches and leave indelible marks on the industry, these key players ensure that the narrative of cryptocurrencies remains as dynamic as the technology itself.

The interplay between technological innovation, economic interests, legal frameworks, and societal adoption underscores the complexity and excitement surrounding cryptocurrency markets. From the conceiving days following Satoshi Nakamoto's whitepaper to the current sprawling market with its diverse participants, the transformation of cryptocurrency from an esoteric concept to a staple of modern finance has been nothing short of revolutionary.

This metamorphosis sets the stage for a deeper examination of the financial, technological, and societal implications of this digital asset phenomenon. The following chapters will delve into the intricate workings of blockchain technology, the different classes of digital currencies, and the strategies one can employ to navigate the cryptocurrency landscape with astute understanding and foresight.

Chapter 2: The Fundamentals of Blockchain Technology

Having taken our first steps into the realm of digital currency, let's now peel back the layers of its underlying engine: blockchain technology. At its core, blockchain is a structure for storing transactional records, commonly known as the block, of the public in several databases, which are known as the "chain," in a network connected through peer-to-peer nodes. Each transaction in this ledger is authorized by the digital signature of the owner. This not only makes it secure but also makes it impossible to manipulate by fraudsters, ensuring its integrity. We'll explore the unique aspects of blockchain, like decentralization and transparency, that make it revolutionary. Imagine a world where transactions are not just secure but also immutable, paving the way for trustless interactions in a digital space where trust is a premium.

At the bedrock of this transformative technology are consensus mechanisms like Proof of Work (PoW) and Proof of Stake (PoS), each with its own set of rules for validation and transaction confirmation, ensuring that all participants agree on the ledger's state. We'll delve into how these mechanisms underpin cryptocurrencies, deterring nefarious actors who might attempt to double-spend or disrupt the network. Furthermore, we shall also consider how smart contracts and decentralized applications (DApps) extend the functionality of blockchains beyond monetary transactions, enabling a multitude of use cases that were previously inconceivable. They're not simply programs; they're self-enforcing agreements embedded into the code that execute when conditions are met, thereby cutting out intermediaries and fostering a new era of decentralized digital services. By understanding these concepts, you'll grasp how blockchain becomes the backbone of a new, unwavering digital architecture that's poised to redefine industries and economies globally.

What Is Blockchain?

he foundation of cryptocurrencies, like Bitcoin and Ethereum, is a technology called blockchain. It's a term that has garnered immense attention and promise beyond digital currencies, impacting sectors from finance to healthcare. But what exactly is blockchain? In essence, this technology is a decentralized database, or ledger, that securely records transactions across numerous computers in such a way that the recorded transactions cannot be altered retroactively.

To understand blockchain, one must first grasp its structure. Think of a blockchain as a series of blocks, where each block contains a number of transactions. Every time a transaction occurs, it's broadcasted to a network of peer-to-peer computers, sometimes referred to as nodes. These nodes then validate the transaction using cryptographic algorithms. Once confirmed to be legitimate, the transaction is clustered with others into a block. Post validation, this block is then added to the chain of previous blocks, hence the term blockchain. This chained structure ensures chronological order and an indelible, transparent transaction history.

One of the defining characteristics of blockchain is its immutability. Once data has been recorded onto a blockchain, it becomes extremely difficult to change. Each block contains its own hash (a unique cryptographic code), and the hash of the previous block in the chain. Changing a single transaction would require changing the entire block's hash, and by extension, every subsequent block, making it nearly impossible to execute without detection.

Blockchain operates on a decentralized network. This means the ledger is not maintained by a single authority, like a bank or government entity, but rather by a distributed network of computers. Decentralization is a fundamental aspect of blockchain's resilience and security, as it removes single points of failure and makes it significantly harder for malicious actors to gain control or alter data.

Transparency is another hallmark of blockchain. Although user identities are encrypted, every transaction is visible to anyone who accesses the blockchain. This promotes a level of accountability and trust that's challenging to achieve with traditional centralized databases.

Blockchain utilizes various consensus mechanisms to agree on the validity of the transactions. The most common among these is Proof of Work (PoW), employed by Bitcoin. However, blockchain's potential stretches far beyond cryptocurrencies, relying on other consensus models like Proof of Stake (PoS) and many variations thereof, which will be detailed further in subsequent sections.

The advent of blockchain technology has also given rise to smart contracts — self-executing contracts with the terms of the agreement between buyer and seller directly written into code. These contracts run on the blockchain and automatically execute actions when certain conditions are met, removing the need for a middleman. This application and others like Decentralized Applications (DApps) will be delved into later, illuminating the versatility and robustness of blockchain.

Blockchain's impact on peer-to-peer transactions cannot be overstated. It enables two parties to exchange assets or information without the need for a trusted third party, which disrupts traditional exchange models. This could potentially reduce transaction times from days to mere minutes and significantly lower transaction costs.

With the concept of digital scarcity, introduced by blockchain, digital assets like cryptocurrencies can now be made finite. This is remarkably different from the digital duplication we frequently see in the digital realm. Each 'coin' or 'token' is unique, which prevents duplication or falsification, ensuring the integrity of the cryptocurrency's value.

Moreover, blockchain's potential for providing solutions in logistics, supply chain management, identity verification, and much more is being actively explored across industries. These ventures strive to capitalize on the strengths of blockchain — enhancing efficiency, security, and traceability of data. The multifaceted applications of this technology will be further explored in later chapters.

Blockchain is also a field of continuous innovation, with ongoing discussions around scalability, energy consumption, and integration into current technological infrastructures. The continuous evolution of blockchain is gathered under an impressive ecosystem of developers, entrepreneurs, and enthusiasts, continually pushing the boundaries of what the technology can achieve.

As readers progress through this book, the intricate workings and nuances of blockchain will become clearer. We'll explore how certain design choices affect network efficiency and security, the trade-offs between different types of blockchains, and how these choices influence their applicability to real-world scenarios.

For aspiring developers and entrepreneurs, blockchain presents a plethora of opportunities to build and innovate. For students, it's an emerging field rich with academic and professional potential. And for investors, understanding the underlying technology is pivotal in making informed decisions about entering and navigating the crypto markets.

In the journey to a deeper comprehension of blockchain, remember that it's as much about grasping the technical underpinnings as it is about seeing blockchain's potential to reshape industries and redefine notions of trust and transparency in the digital age.

As the sections to follow build upon the foundation of blockchain knowledge, they will also serve to elucidate the transformative nature of this technology, empower readers with the capacity to envision future applications, and provide the analytical tools to discern the many opportunities and challenges that come with adopting blockchain and cryptocurrencies.

Consensus Mechanisms: PoW, PoS, and Beyond

The journey through the realm of blockchain technology leads us to a critical juncture: understanding how decentralized networks achieve agreement, oftentimes referred to as consensus. Consensus mechanisms are core to the functionality of these networks, as they are the means by which all participants can agree on the state of the ledger, even in the absence of trust among parties. For aspirants exploring the depths of blockchain technology, grasping how consensus mechanisms work can provide insightful perspectives into not just how cryptocurrencies function, but also their broader implications in the digital economy.

Proof of Work (PoW), as pioneered by Bitcoin, lays the groundwork for consensus on the blockchain. In this system, miners compete to solve complex mathematical puzzles using computational power. The first to solve the puzzle gets the right to add a new block to the blockchain and is rewarded with cryptocurrency. This mechanism ensures security since rewriting the ledger would require vast amounts of computational power, making it impractical to carry out a fraudulent transaction. However, the energy-intensive nature of PoW has been a source of concern, as it demands significant amounts of electricity, leading to critiques over environmental impact.

The quest for scalability and energy efficiency has led to the second most well-known consensus mechanism: Proof of Stake (PoS). Unlike PoW, PoS awards the creation of new blocks to validators based on the number of coins they hold and are willing to "stake" as collateral. The higher the stake, the higher the chances of being selected as a validator. This model reduces the amount of computational work required to verify transactions, thereby slashing electricity consumption and allowing greater scalability.

Within PoS, there's also a concept known as 'Forging' or 'Minting'. This process is inherently similar to mining but without the extreme use of computational power. Validators are selected to create a block based on various combinations of random selection and wealth or age (the stake).

Furthermore, within the PoS umbrella, there are variations like Delegated Proof of Stake (DPoS), where stakeholders vote for a few delegates who secure the network on their behalf. This can further increase the scalability by reducing the number of nodes necessary for consensus and quicken the pace of transactions; however, it often leads to concerns about centralization, as fewer nodes have more power.

Hybrid models have also emerged. For example, some blockchain networks employ both PoW and PoS, using the best attributes of each to optimize security and efficiency. These systems can use the Proof of Work mechanism to mine initial blocks, but over time, as the network matures, it switches over to Proof of Stake.

Looking beyond PoW and PoS, newer mechanisms such as Proof of Authority (PoA) and Proof of Burn (PoB) explore different ways to ensure network agreement while addressing the limitations of their predecessors. PoA relies on known and reputable validators to validate transactions, tailoring to private blockchains or consortiums where trust is placed in these authorities. PoB invites participants to 'burn' some of their tokens, removing them from circulation to gain the right to add a block to the blockchain, symbolizing a long-term commitment to the network's coin.

It's important to highlight Directed Acyclic Graph (DAG) technology as well, which is employed by projects like IOTA. DAG systems have participants directly confirm previous transactions in order to conduct their own, thus eliminating the need for miners or stakers and allowing for rapid transaction processing.

These advancements in consensus mechanisms enhance not only transaction speeds and energy efficiency but also broaden our understanding of how distributed systems can operate. As these mechanisms evolve, they will likely unlock new possibilities for building decentralized applications (DApps) and conducting transactions.

For developers, understanding these mechanisms is akin to understanding the engine of a car. Having this knowledge allows for better design choices when creating applications on top of the blockchain. Investors, on the other hand, can infer the potential longevity and sustainability of various cryptocurrency projects based on the underlying mechanisms employed.

At this crossroads, it's pivotal for all involved to understand where PoW and PoS are taking us and to harness the potential of what lies beyond. The future of blockchain technology and its myriad applications depends greatly on these consensus mechanisms, their continued development, and the balance they strike between decentralization, security, and environmental sustainability.

Embracing this technology requires us to be both curious and critical, examining not just the 'how' but also the 'why' behind these consensus mechanisms. Educating oneself about the principles and practice of PoW, PoS, and emerging alternatives is not just prudent — it's essential for anyone serious about participating meaningfully in the cryptocurrency and blockchain space.

While consensus mechanisms may seem like an arcane topic, they are integral to our understanding of how trust, agreement, and security are engineered in a digital world. As we move forward, the stage is set for innovative consensus algorithms that could catalyze the next wave of blockchain evolution, pushing us towards a more integrated and efficient digital economy.

In summary, consensus mechanisms are the beating heart of blockchain technology, driving the pulse of every cryptocurrency and decentralized network. By delving into PoW, PoS, and the novel consensus mechanisms on the horizon, we can better equip ourselves for the opportunities and challenges that await in the fast-evolving world of blockchain and cryptocurrency.

Smart Contracts and DApps

The term "smart contract" might evoke the image of a legal document imbued with artificial intelligence. While not quite AI, smart contracts are, in essence, self-executing contracts where the terms of the agreement are directly written into lines of code. The beauty of smart contracts is their ability to automate and decentralize processes that traditionally would require intermediaries, such as banks or lawyers, to validate and enforce.

The blockchain, an immutable and distributed ledger, serves as the backbone for smart contracts, providing a platform where these digital agreements can operate securely and transparently. This immutability ensures that once a smart contract is deployed to the blockchain, it cannot be altered, reducing the potential for fraud and bringing a new level of trust to digital transactions.

Smart contracts can be thought of as digital vending machines. If you meet the defined criteria or feed the machine what it asks for, it dispenses the goods without any need for human intervention. In a similar way, once a smart contract's conditions are met, it automatically executes the agreed-upon actions, such as releasing funds or registering a title.

Now, let's explore decentralized applications, or DApps for short. DApps are applications that run on a peer-to-peer network of computers rather than a single computer. They are the complex form of smart contract usage, designed with the intention to serve broader domains of utility beyond single transactions. A DApp can consist of one or many interconnected smart contracts, working together to create a fully fledged application.

The power of DApps is they operate in a trustless and tamper-proof ecosystem provided by blockchain. Unlike traditional apps, DApps give users a level of assurance that their data is not being manipulated and that the rules of the application cannot be changed without the consensus of the community.

This unique aspect of decentralized applications is revolutionizing various industries. In the realm of finance, DApps are enabling peer-to-peer lending and borrowing, creating transparent and inclusive financial services without intermediaries. They're fostering the growth of "DeFi" or decentralized finance, which is challenging the traditional financial sector through automated, permissionless financial services that operate on blockchain technology.

Another key area thriving on DApps is gaming. Blockchain-based games leverage smart contracts to create in-game economies where players truly own their assets as non-fungible tokens (NFTs), and can trade them in markets that are fair and transparent.

In terms of development, creating a DApp shares similarities with building a traditional web application but requires additional components to interact with the blockchain. Developers must craft both the front-end user experience and the back-end blockchain logic. Popular blockchain platforms for developing DApps include Ethereum, EOS, and Tron, each offering different levels of complexity, scalability, and community support.

DApps are also gaining traction due to the incentivization they offer to users and developers. Many DApps have their own native tokens, rewarding users for participation or contributing computational power to the network. By aligning incentives among all parties involved, DApps can grow organically and sustainably.

For investors in the cryptocurrency space, understanding smart contracts and DApps is crucial. Not only do they form the core utility of many tokens, but they also represent the practical realization of blockchain's promise. By investing in tokens of DApps or platforms that facilitate smart contracts, one isn't just betting on digital currencies but moreover on the underlying digital economies that stand to disrupt traditional business models.

When analyzing DApps or smart contract platforms for investment, it's important to consider the developer community around them. A vibrant developer ecosystem usually signals an ongoing innovation and maintenance, which are vital for the long-term success of a technology platform.

Furthermore, with the smart contract code being open for scrutiny, security becomes a paramount concern. It's not uncommon for bugs in smart contracts to lead to substantial financial losses. Therefore, security audits and a strong reputation for robust code are essential factors to weigh when evaluating potential investments.

User adoption is another pivotal factor. A DApp may have revolutionary technology, but if it's too complex or doesn't resolve a significant pain point, it will struggle to gain traction. User-friendly interfaces and clear value propositions are what separate widely adopted DApps from those that languish in obscurity.

Smart contracts and DApps form a symbiotic relationship within the blockchain ecosystem, where one enables the other. While smart contracts provide the secure and reliable environment for transactions, DApps give users accessible ways to harness this innovative technology. Together, they're reshaping how we interact with digital services, laying the groundwork for an intriguing future where decentralization is the norm.

The exploration of smart contracts and DApps sheds light on the intricate dance between technology and user adoption. It's a vibrant field that is not just theoretical but is seeing practical and impactful applications across industries. For anyone looking to delve into cryptocurrencies or blockchain, understanding these concepts is not just recommended; it's essential. They epitomize the perfect blend of innovation and practicality, symbolizing a robust pillar within the ever-evolving digital landscape of blockchain technology.

Chapter 3: Decoding Cryptocurrency: Bitcoin and Altcoins

As we transition from the groundbreaking mechanism of blockchain covered in the previous chapter, it's essential to grasp the diverse landscape of cryptocurrencies that leverages this technology. Bitcoin emerged as the trailblazer, a beacon of decentralization, challenging conventional monetary systems and paving the way for 'digital gold'. However, the real thrill lies in the labyrinth of 'altcoins', each with unique attributes, communities, and use cases that push the frontiers of what digital money can mean. Among them, titans like Ethereum introduced functionalities that extend far beyond simple transactions, shaping new economies surrounding Initial Coin Offerings (ICOs) and tokens. This chapter unfolds the enigmatic world of Bitcoin and its alternative counterparts, shining a light on the intricate fabric that empowers you to navigate this complex tapestry of digital assets. By understanding the distinct features and the evolutionary trajectory of these coins, investors and enthusiasts can make informed decisions, leveraging the dynamic potentialities that lie within cryptocurrency.

Introduction to Bitcoin

As we delve further into the world of digital currency, it's imperative to focus on the archetype of cryptocurrencies: Bitcoin. It's essential to understand Bitcoin not only as a digital asset but as the innovative technology that spearheaded an entirely new financial epoch. In this introduction, expect to unfold the layers that define Bitcoin, providing you a solid foundation before exploring the vast expanse of cryptocurrency.

Bitcoin is often referred to as digital gold, and rightly so, due to its ability to preserve and increase value over time. This isn't an imaginary concept but rests on real principles and technology. Bitcoin runs on a decentralized ledger called blockchain, ensuring transparency, security, and immutability. These attributes lead Bitcoin to often be the first choice for newcomers venturing into the crypto realm.

To fully appreciate Bitcoin, let's embark on a brief journey through its origins. It was in 2008 when an entity – known by the pseudonym Satoshi Nakamoto – published the Bitcoin whitepaper. This document laid the foundation for a peer-to-peer electronic cash system, which was revolutionary in its proposal to eliminate the need for central authorities like banks.

The first block, known as the genesis block, was mined by Nakamoto in January 2009, marking the birth of the Bitcoin network. This was more than just technical achievement; it was a political statement about financial sovereignty. Each Bitcoin transaction since that day has been recorded on the blockchain, a testament to a functioning decentralized system.

Underpinning Bitcoin is the proof-of-work consensus mechanism, which secures the network and validates transactions. This system relies on miners, individuals and companies who use computational power to solve complex mathematical puzzles. Successful mining not only validates and records transactions but also mints new bitcoins as a reward, an intriguing concept known as mining.

The finite supply of Bitcoin is another distinctive feature. There are only 21 million bitcoins that can ever exist, mirroring the scarcity and value proposition of gold. This limitation stands in stark contrast to fiat currencies, which central banks can inflate indefinitely. This coded scarcity plays a significant role in Bitcoin's investment narrative.

Engaging with Bitcoin starts by setting up a digital wallet. This electronic wallet is secured with a unique private key, which you must safeguard diligently. Your wallet address serves as a public key, similar to an account number, allowing you to send and receive bitcoins. Transactions on the network are nearly instantaneous and can be viewed publicly on the blockchain, offering transparency like never before.

Bitcoin's rise in value and acceptance amongst the general population has been meteoric. What began as an obscure, technical intrigue is now a widely acknowledged store of value. Its acceptance ranges from individual investors to institutions, and even some governments consider it an asset class worth holding.

Understanding Bitcoin involves not just grasping its technical underpinnings but also recognizing its impact on the global financial system. As the forerunner of decentralized digital currencies, Bitcoin has paved the way for discussions about financial autonomy, privacy, and the role of traditional financial institutions.

Bitcoin's journey hasn't been without its share of volatility. Prices can swing dramatically, influenced by regulatory news, technical developments, and market sentiment. And yet, despite its turbulent nature, Bitcoin has persisted as a beacon of what blockchain technology can achieve, and continues to attract investment.

The role of Bitcoin within the economic landscape has also evolved. While originally conceived as a medium of exchange, its current utilitarian role is more akin to a digital savings instrument. The potential for high returns has made it an attractive investment opportunity, though it comes with high risks that should be well understood.

Moreover, Bitcoin has shaped the conversation around financial privacy and autonomy. As individuals have grown wary of centralized control over money, Bitcoin offers an alternative that aligns with a vision of personal freedom and resistance to censorship.

Finally, entering the world of Bitcoin means joining a vibrant community that spans developers, investors, enthusiasts, and skeptics. This community is constantly pushing the boundaries of technology, debating economic principles, and envisioning a future that is increasingly decentralized.

In sum, Bitcoin is more than just another asset; it is a movement, a philosophy, and a benchmark in the financial technology space. As we explore its intricacies and understand its potential, we're not just learning about a cryptocurrency but also about monumental shifts in how we perceive and engage with value in a digital age.

To understand Bitcoin is to equip oneself with knowledge that is foundational for navigating the future of money. While we will touch upon investing, technology, and security in subsequent chapters, this grounding in Bitcoin will serve as your compass in the burgeoning landscape of cryptocurrencies. Be aware of its potential, mindful of its volatility, and appreciative of its technology as we continue our journey through the cryptoverse.

Exploring Altcoins: Ethereum, Litecoin, and More

As you've become more familiar with Bitcoin through the early chapters, it's now time to broaden your horizon and set your sights on the diverse landscape of altcoins. Standing for 'alternative coins,' altcoins are cryptocurrencies other than Bitcoin. They offer varied use cases, technological advancements, or consensus mechanisms that differentiate them from Bitcoin's pioneering design. This chapter aims to illuminate the colorful spectrum of leading altcoins, exploring their unique offerings and potential impact on the future of digital currency.

In this foray into altcoins, Ethereum often takes the spotlight as the first successor of Bitcoin not, merely by market cap, but by its novel contribution to blockchain technology. Ethereum introduced smart contracts, self-executing contracts with the terms of the agreement directly written into code. This innovation has not only expanded the application of blockchain technology beyond simple transactions but has also paved the way for decentralized applications (DApps) to be built atop its platform.

Ethereum's prominence is not accidental but the result of its robust capabilities in enabling developers to craft programmable decentralization. This altcoin has successfully attracted an engaged community of developers and enthusiasts who are inventing new ways to harness the power of the blockchain. With Ethereum, we can envisage a world where decentralized finance (DeFi) applications unlock liquidity and financial services for everyone, irrespective of geographic and institutional boundaries.

The next altcoin on our exploration is Litecoin, often referred to as the silver to Bitcoin's gold. Created by Charlie Lee in 2011, Litecoin is a peer-to-peer cryptocurrency inspired by Bitcoin, with primary distinctions in its hashing algorithm, hard cap, block transaction times, and other minor differentiations. Though initially conceived to be a lighter version that could offer faster transaction times and lower fees, Litecoin's wider implications have ushered in a significant following and acceptance by merchants and consumers alike.

Litecoin's expedited transaction confirmation times make it an appealing option for users who require quicker transaction processing and merchants who seek fast settlement for their goods and services. As you know, speed and efficiency are crucial in commerce, and Litecoin has carved out a niche in the space where rapid transaction throughput is highly valued.

Yet, the world of altcoins extends well beyond Ethereum and Litecoin, encompassing a multitude of ambitious projects seeking to resolve distinct market needs. Take, for instance, Ripple (XRP), a digital payment protocol that diverges from the typical blockchain model to facilitate lightning-fast and cost-effective cross-border money transfers for banks and financial institutions.

Ripple's target audience is starkly different from most cryptocurrencies that cater to retail investors or aim to solve consumer-centric problems. Instead, Ripple aims to embed itself as an essential facilitator within the existing financial system rather than position itself as its outright replacement. This sets an interesting precedent, demonstrating the varied directions innovative altcoins can take.

It's important to note that the altcoin space is vast and volatile, with new coins and tokens emerging regularly through Initial Coin Offerings (ICOs) and other launch mechanisms. Each altcoin comes with its unique parameters, use cases, and community support. Some aim to improve upon Bitcoin's features, while others venture into entirely new realms such as governance, cloud storage, or even digital identity verification.

Cardano (ADA), for example, stands out among altcoins with its emphasis on peer-reviewed scientific research as the foundation for building its technology. Its layered architecture is designed for scalability and the facilitation of smart contracts and decentralized applications with a high level of security. The Cardano project, led by one of Ethereum's co-founders, underlines the value of a measured, research-based approach to innovation in the cryptosphere.

When diving into the altcoin sea, it is, however, imperative to approach with caution. For every legitimate project, there are scores of others with less scrupulous intentions or questionable value propositions. It is vital for any investor or enthusiast to conduct thorough research, leveraging a multitude of resources such as white-papers, community forums, and financial analyses to discern the potential and legitimacy of a given altcoin.

Investment in altcoins requires not only financial acumen but technical understanding. It is the intricate dance between market dynamics and blockchain technology that will determine the success and longevity of any altcoin in a market brimming with competition and innovation.

As we go on, remember that while Bitcoin is the progenitor of this digital currency movement, the altcoins that follow are charting paths that could lead to profound changes in various industries and societal structures. Contributors to blockchain technology and crypto-currencies are no longer just starting revolutions in financial systems, they are redefining what it means to exchange value and trust in a rapidly digitizing world.

Thus, Ethereum, Litecoin, and the plethora of altcoins are not merely digital assets to consider for portfolios; they are harbingers of a coming age that sees decentralized applications and services as commonplace. They challenge us to reimagine the world with fewer central points of control, heightened transparency, and increased efficiency in every digital interaction.

For aspiring developers, entrepreneurs, and students, this ecosystem presents a fecund ground for innovation. It's a vibrant laboratory where monetary theory, computer science, and social dynamics intersect to create unprecedented opportunities for those willing to learn and experiment.

Through exploration and education, individuals can better position themselves to both contribute to and capitalize on this still-nascent industry. It's a rare moment in human history where the barriers to entry are low enough for individual participation to potentially shape global economic and technological landscapes.

Investors need to recognize that the altcoin universe is dynamic and that the importance of diligence cannot be overstated. In an industry where change is the only constant, keeping abreast of technological advancements, community sentiment, and regulatory shifts is essential. Each altcoin represents not just a potential financial investment but also a stake in the possible futures being crafted through distributed ledger technology.

In the realm of cryptocurrency, knowledge truly is power, and as we have seen, power is increasingly defined by one's grasp of digital currencies and the blockchain. By understanding the varied offerings of altcoins like Ethereum, Litecoin, and the many emerging players, one stands at the cusp of the next technological frontier — prepared to seize the opportunities that lie within.

ICOs, Tokens, and the New Digital Assets

A groundbreaking innovation of the cryptocurrency world, often not fully understood by newcomers, is the creation of initial coin offerings (ICOs), tokens, and other digital assets. These instruments have emerged as a powerful means of fundraising and have helped forge a completely new economic landscape.

Let's dive into ICOs first. An ICO is essentially a crowdfunding event that uses cryptocurrencies. New projects sell their underlying crypto tokens to raise capital and fund the development of their platforms. Think of it as the blockchain equivalent of an IPO (Initial Public Offering) in the stock market, with some key differences – mainly that it's relatively accessible; individuals around the world can participate, sometimes without substantial funds or traditional investment accreditation.

During an ICO, investors purchase tokens, which often grant them access to the services a platform aims to provide, or a stake in the project itself. However, a token's value can fluctuate wildly after an ICO, based on factors like project success, user adoption, and market sentiment, thus carrying significant risks for investors.

Tokens are the lifeblood of these ecosystems. They aren't just a currency; they can embody a diverse range of assets and functions. Utility tokens, for example, grant holders a right to use certain features of a project once it's deployed. On the other hand, security tokens represent investment contracts and often emulate traditional securities, promising dividends or ownership rights.

The emergence of tokenized assets has opened the door to a new realm of possibilities. Real-world assets like real estate, art, and even intellectual property can now be represented by digital tokens on the blockchain. This process provides more fluidity and accessibility to otherwise illiquid markets, and it transcends geographic borders.

Despite the excitement surrounding new digital assets, navigating the ICO and token landscape requires due diligence. Not all projects succeed, and the field is rife with examples of overpromises and under-delivery, sometimes even outright scams. It is crucial to thoroughly research a project's team, vision, technical feasibility, and community support before investing.

Regulatory considerations also play a significant role in the ICO arena. Since the rise of ICOs, regulators around the world, such as the SEC in the United States, have been catching up to impose measures to protect investors. These regulations ensure that token issuances comply with financial laws, effectively precluding fraudulent activities.

The explosion of ICOs has also introduced novel funding mechanisms within the token economy. For instance, Simple Agreements for Future Tokens (SAFT) are contracts that allow investors to purchase tokens before they are minted, often at a discount, with the caveat that they will receive the tokens once the project launches.

It's also imperative to consider the technical and economic models of tokens. For example, does the token have a fixed supply, or is it inflationary? How is the token distributed? These factors can have profound implications for the scarcity, and potential value, of a token over time.

ICOs and tokens have also spurred innovation in the types of platforms that can be funded. Decentralized autonomous organizations (DAOs), DeFi (decentralized finance) platforms, and NFT (non-fungible token) marketplaces have all been birthed through this new funding model. They've turned speculative ideas into living, breathing ecosystems that are disrupting traditional industries.

One of the most crucial aspects of ICOs, overlooked by many, is the community. A strong, active, and engaged community can be a significant asset for any project. Community members often become advocates, developers, and early adopters, driving the project forward through network effects.

Furthermore, ICOs have inspired a meritocratic ethos within the cryptocurrency space. Good projects can rise to the top based on their technical merit, innovation, and community support, not just on the depth of their creators' pockets or their marketing prowess.

In terms of investment strategies, tokens represent both opportunity and a high risk. Proper portfolio management – never investing more than one can afford to lose, diversifying investments, and tracking market conditions – should be followed. One notable strategy is participating in ICOs with the potential to provide early access to promising technologies before they hit public exchanges.

Lastly, the token economy is evolving rapidly, and so is its lexicon. Terms like "IEO" (Initial Exchange Offering) have emerged, where exchanges conduct the ICO on behalf of projects, providing instant liquidity to the tokens once the offering is over. Another is STO (Security Token Offering), focusing on issuing regulated securities on the blockchain. This lexicon reflects the innovation and iteration speed within the field.

In conclusion, ICOs, tokens, and new digital assets are creating a dynamic and ever-shifting investment landscape. Potential investors should educate themselves, stay informed about technological and regulatory developments, and approach opportunities with a mix of enthusiasm and caution. It's a vibrant, untapped world with the potential for significant returns and, importantly, a nursery where nascent ideas can transform into the foundational technologies of tomorrow.

Chapter 4:
Investing in Cryptocurrencies: First Steps

If you've journeyed thus far into the heart of cryptocurrency, you're likely eager to take the tangible leap into investing. The first stride is establishing a secure digital wallet—a custodian for your digital assets that blends security with accessibility. Selecting the correct wallet is a delicate dance of personal needs and security features, and it is your primary tool in the crypto ecosystem. Then, you'll venture onto exchanges and trading platforms, the bustling marketplaces of digital currency. Here, informed choices on platform reputability and liquidity become your guiding stars. Your inaugural transaction isn't merely a trade; it's a rite of passage in this paradigm shift of wealth exchange. It represents a bridge between traditional financial understanding and the emergent digital economy. As you stand at the threshold, remember investing is not just about capital—it's about cultivating wisdom in the art of the future's currency. Embrace this venture with both caution and curiosity, for while the steps are straightforward, the path is uncharted, and each footprint you leave is integral to forging your distinct journey through the crypto cosmos.

Setting Up Your Digital Wallet

Entering the world of cryptocurrency requires a fundamental tool—the digital wallet. This storage solution is pivotal for anyone aspiring to buy, sell, or hold digital currencies. Navigating through various wallet options and security measures might seem daunting, but understanding your digital wallet's functionality is as important as grasping the intricacies of the currencies themselves. Like securing a vault, setting up your digital wallet is about creating a safe space for your digital assets.

A digital wallet operates as a private interface to a user's cryptocurrency holdings, connecting to the blockchain where the assets live. Unlike a physical wallet, which holds your cash or cards, a digital wallet doesn't store currency tangibly. Instead, it securely saves your cryptographic keys—public and private keys that are the essence of accessing and transacting with your cryptocurrency.

The first step in setting up your digital wallet is choosing the right type based on your needs. Wallets can be hot or cold, software or hardware. Hot wallets are connected to the internet and offer ease of use and quick access, making them suitable for everyday transactions and trading. However, they may be more susceptible to online threats. Conversely, cold wallets are offline, such as hardware wallets or paper wallets, granting a higher level of security and are often favored for storing large amounts of cryptocurrencies long-term.

Software wallets are applications you can download on your desktop or mobile device. These are generally free and user-friendly, allowing you to swiftly execute transactions. Mobile wallets, in particular, offer the convenience of managing your crypto on the go. However, the security of software wallets is only as strong as the device's security, so it's crucial to have robust anti-virus and anti-malware systems in place.

Hardware wallets, on the other hand, are physical devices that store your keys offline. Even though they require a monetary investment, they're less vulnerable to hacking since they disconnect from the internet when not in use. The setup process for hardware wallets typically includes initializing the device, creating a secure pin, and noting down the recovery phrase critical for backing up your wallet.

The recovery phrase, also known as a seed phrase, is a series of words generated by your wallet that grants you access to your cryptocurrencies. This phrase is of utmost importance as it's the only way to recover your funds if you lose access to your wallet. Write it down on paper, store it in a safe place, and never share it with anyone. Some individuals go as far as to store multiple copies in different locations for added security.

Once you've written down your recovery phrase and stored it securely, you'll want to receive your first transaction. You can do this by sharing your public key, or wallet address, which is akin to an account number, with the sender. Unlike the private key, the public key can be shared without risk, as it only allows others to send funds to your wallet.

For high-value transactions, or if you're planning to hold significant amounts of cryptocurrency, multi-signature wallets add an extra layer of security. These require multiple private keys to authorize a cryptocurrency transaction. This method is especially useful for businesses or groups where funds should only move with collective approval.

It's not uncommon for newcomers to worry about the safety of their digital assets, but remember that many security breaches are due to user error. Always double-check wallet addresses before sending or receiving funds, and be wary of phishing sites and suspicious emails that may attempt to gain access to your wallet. Employing strong, unique passwords and enabling two-factor authentication (2FA) whenever possible will also increase security.

Familiarize yourself with the backup and restore processes of your chosen wallet. Such knowledge can make a critical difference in situations where devices are lost, stolen or damaged. Understand that in the realm of cryptocurrency, personal responsibility is key; there's no bank to call for a forgotten password or unauthorized transaction.

Maintenance is also crucial. Software updates for wallets often contain security enhancements and bug fixes. Ensure that you're running the latest version of your wallet's software to protect against new threats. Additionally, reviewing your wallet's activity regularly helps you to recognize any unauthorized actions quickly, allowing you to take prompt measures.

As you gain confidence and expand your activities in the cryptocurrency ecosystem, you might consider using different wallets for different purposes—such as having a mobile wallet for daily spending and a hardware wallet for savings. Managing multiple wallets does mean managing multiple sets of keys, so organization and security practices become even more vital.

To those taking their first steps into cryptocurrency, setting up your digital wallet may summon both excitement and trepidation. The financial sovereignty it brings also comes with the full weight of protecting your digital wealth. Approach this responsibility with attentive caution, and view each measure you adopt—be it security practices or backup routines—as an investment in your financial future.

When you've successfully set up and secured your digital wallet, you are ready to embark on a journey of transactions, investments, and perhaps even a foray into the endless possibilities of decentralized applications and smart contracts. Your wallet is more than a tool; it's the gateway to an innovative financial landscape that you are now a part of. As you continue to learn and grow within this space, keep updating your knowledge along with your wallet, ensuring that both are well-equipped for the journey ahead in the ever-evolving world of cryptocurrency.

Exchanges and Trading Platforms

As our journey into the world of cryptocurrency investing advances, we now turn to the vibrant hubs where digital assets come alive – the exchanges and trading platforms. These are the digital marketplaces where individuals can buy, sell, or trade cryptocurrencies. This critical part of the crypto ecosystem functions much like traditional stock exchanges, though there are some key differences that need to be outlined.

First and foremost, let's define what a cryptocurrency exchange is. It's a platform that facilitates the trading of cryptocurrencies for other assets, including digital and fiat currencies. This is the cornerstone of your trading journey; choosing the right platform can make a significant impact on your experience and success.

There are two primary types of exchanges: centralized and decentralized. Centralized exchanges (CEX) are managed by a company that provides a platform for users to trade. They tend to be user-friendly and are a common entry point for beginners due to their ease of use and customer support. However, they can be considered less secure as they present a centralized point of potential failure, and users do not have control of their private keys.

On the other hand, Decentralized exchanges (DEX) operate without a central authority and allow users to execute peer-to-peer transactions directly. This removes the risk of a single point of failure and gives users full control over their funds. However, they can be more complex to navigate and might lack the liquidity of their centralized counterparts.

Liquidity is vital to a healthy exchange environment. It means that there are enough market participants buying and selling to ensure that trades can be executed quickly and at stable prices. High liquidity facilitates better price discovery and allows for larger volumes of trades without significantly affecting the market price.

Security is paramount in choosing an exchange. It's crucial to pick a platform that employs robust security measures to protect your assets. Many leading exchanges implement measures such as two-factor authentication (2FA), cold storage of funds, and insurance policies to safeguard against hacks and thefts.

Fees are another important consideration. Trading platforms typically charge fees for transactions. These can include trading fees, withdrawal fees, and sometimes deposit fees. It's essential to understand the fee structure of an exchange, as this can impact the overall profitability of your trading activities.

User experience can not be overlooked. For a beginner, the user interface should be intuitive and easy to navigate. Features like real-time charts, order books, and trade history should be accessible to facilitate informed trading decisions.

Then there's customer support. The availability and quality of customer service can be a deal-breaker for many users. In a world where technical glitches can potentially mean the loss of funds, responsive and helpful customer support is crucial.

Another essential feature to consider is the range of available cryptocurrencies. While most of the exchanges offer popular coins like Bitcoin and Ethereum, if you're interested in less known or newer altcoins, you'll need to find platforms that list these assets.

Insurance funds are becoming a popular feature amongst some of the more established exchanges. These funds are designed to protect customers against potential losses that could occur should the platform experience a breach or failure.

Some platforms also offer additional services such as staking, lending, or even derivative trading. Staking allows users to earn rewards by holding certain cryptocurrencies, while lending offers the opportunity to earn interest on crypto assets lent out to others.

When choosing a platform, it's also wise to consider its geographical restrictions. Some exchanges may not operate or may limit services in certain countries due to local regulations. Always ensure that the chosen platform is available and compliant in your region.

With knowledge of these exchanges and platforms, you're now better equipped to embark on your trading journey. Moreover, always remember that due diligence is a critical step before committing to an exchange. It's important to perform thorough research, read reviews, and, if possible, test the platform with a small amount of money before fully diving in.

Finally, continuous education on the workings of exchanges and the ever-changing landscape of the cryptocurrency market will greatly enhance your skills as a trader. The ability to navigate these platforms with confidence and savvy will serve as a significant asset in your investment endeavors.

As we move beyond the mechanics of exchanges and dive deeper into the act of trading itself, remember that the choice of where to trade is just as important as what you trade. So, arm yourself with knowledge, stay updated, and approach exchanges with a strategic mindset. This will lay down a solid foundation for success in the dynamic and exciting realm of cryptocurrency investing.

Conducting Your First Transaction

After exploring digital wallets and familiarizing yourself with the diverse landscape of exchanges, you're ready to embark on a new rite of passage within the cryptocurrency realm: conducting your first transaction. This process is not only a technical endeavor, but it also symbolizes your entry into a global community dedicated to financial sovereignty and innovation.

First, ensure that you have completed the necessary preliminary steps – setting up a digital wallet and selecting a reputable exchange or trading platform. Your digital wallet will be the point from which you send or receive cryptocurrencies, and the exchange is your gateway to the market.

Begin by depositing funds into your exchange account. This could be done through bank transfers, credit card payments, or even by using other cryptocurrencies. It's important to understand the fees associated with each method, as they might affect your transaction decisions. Once your funds are available, you'll be ready to purchase your first cryptocurrency.

When buying crypto, you'll encounter the concepts of 'market' and 'limit' orders. A market order will purchase the cryptocurrency instantly at the current market price, while a limit order allows you to set a specific price at which you're willing to buy or sell. As a beginner, it might be easier to start with a market order to get a feel for the process.

Navigate the exchange's interface to select the cryptocurrency you wish to purchase. You'll see an order book displaying current buy and sell orders – a vivid example of how crypto markets are alive with the energy of global trades.

Enter the amount of cryptocurrency you want to buy and execute your market order. Within moments, you'll witness the first addition to your digital wallet, a momentous step that shouldn't be underestimated for its simplicity.

Once you've made your purchase, it is imperative to transfer your new assets from the exchange to your private wallet. Maintaining control of your private keys is a fundamental best practice in cryptocurrency – it ensures your holdings are not overly exposed to the risks associated with exchange platforms.

To transfer your coins to your wallet, locate the 'withdraw' function on the exchange. You will need to enter your wallet's public address. Double-check this address; sending to the wrong address could result in an irreversible loss of funds. With the address entered correctly, initiate the withdrawal.

The transaction will now be broadcasted to the network and included in the next available block, pending miners' confirmation. Depending on the cryptocurrency and the network's congestion, this could take from a few minutes to an hour – sometimes more. Patience is vital at this stage.

Once the transaction has been confirmed, your private wallet's balance should reflect the new amount. Congratulations, you've now completed your first crypto transaction – taking you from a mere spectator to an active participant in the relentless evolution of the digital economy.

This act of transferring value, almost magical in its execution, is more than just an exchange of currency. It's a testament to the power of blockchain technology and the vast potential it holds to redefine financial interactions across the globe.

Keep in mind, with every transaction you engage in, you're not only reinforcing your technical understanding but also growing more deeply interconnected with the economic and social dimensions of cryptocurrency. Each trade, each transfer, each smart decision builds your confidence and expanse of knowledge.

While early transactions may be simple, they pave the way for more complex dealings, such as participating in ICOs, using decentralized exchanges, or engaging in peer-to-peer transactions. Every step is a building block in your journey to becoming a seasoned participant in the world of blockchain.

Take a moment to reflect on this milestone. You've now joined countless others in the promise of a new financial future, underpinned by technology that is open, borderless, and inclusive. Embrace the continuous learning curve, and let your first transaction be the foundation of an enlightened path in this revolutionary digital space.

And so, as you venture forth, remember that each transaction will yield valuable insights. Stay informed, practice diligent security measures, and maintain a mindset ready for growth. The secret to mastery in this space doesn't lie in a single grand action, but in the cumulative power of many deliberate, one calculated transaction at a time.

Chapter 5: Developing an Investor Mindset

Building upon the initial foray into cryptocurrency transactions, we pivot towards cultivating a strategic mental framework essential for investment longevity. Crafting an investor mindset is not merely about analytical prowess—it's about resilience, adaptability, and a meticulous approach to risk. This chapter serves as a linchpin for aspiring investors, introducing them to the pillars of sound judgment and tactical thinking that characterize seasoned market participants. It unlocks the essence of risk management in a volatile market, steering clear from emotional decision-making and focusing on rational evaluation of market forces. Through portfolio diversification, one learns to weave a safety net that sustains gains and buffers falls, ensuring that all eggs aren't perilously placed in one basket. As one's journey in the cryptocurrency labyrinth advances, the profound significance of analytical tools in discerning market trends becomes undeniable, molding a mindset geared towards long-term prosperity. Embrace the intricacies of these disciplines, and you'll find that developing an investor mindset isn't just about accruing wealth—it's about forging a sustainable path through the digital financial frontier.

Risk Management in Cryptocurrency Investing

Investing in cryptocurrencies can be an exhilarating journey, filled with immense potential for profit but equally fraught with risks. It's essential for investors, especially those new to the digital currency space, to understand and implement robust risk management strategies. Managing risk is the backbone of a successful investment mindset and key to long-term sustainability in the volatile world of cryptocurrencies.

Risk management in cryptocurrency investing involves identifying, assessing, and prioritizing risks followed by coordinated and economical application of resources to minimize, control, and monitor the probability or impact of unfortunate events. A mature approach includes diversifying investments, setting clear goals, employing stop-loss orders, and continuously educating oneself about market trends and new technologies.

First and foremost, investors should never invest more money than they can afford to lose. The cryptocurrency market is known for its sharp and sudden fluctuations, which can result in significant losses. Diversification is a powerful tool in the arsenal of an investor. Instead of pouring all funds into a single asset, spreading investments across various types of assets can reduce overall risk.

Understanding one's own risk tolerance is crucial. Each investor has a different capacity for risk, driven by factors like income, investment goals, time horizons, and personality. Knowing where you stand on the risk spectrum helps in crafting a balanced and appropriate investment strategy. It's about finding that sweet spot where the potential for growth aligns with one's peace of mind.

Setting clear investment goals with attainable targets can also act as a guide through the tumultuous crypto market. Whether it's achieving a certain return on investment (ROI), building a nest egg, or sup-orting innovative technology projects, goals help to maintain focus and not be swayed by market hysteria. They serve as a reminder to investors to take profits when possible and reevaluate positions when necessary.

Another fundamental risk management practice involves setting stop-loss orders. A stop-loss is an order placed with a broker to sell a security when it reaches a certain price. This tool aids in preventing large losses in the event of a sudden downturn. It is an integral part of trading discipline, allowing investors to set their loss thresholds in advance.

Continuous education is also an essential element in managing risk. The cryptocurrency space evolves rapidly with new coins, technologies, regulations, and security risks emerging regularly. Staying informed about these changes can help investors avoid potential pitfalls and make more calculated investment decisions.

Diligent research into what you're investing in cannot be overstated. Before adding an asset to your portfolio, conduct a thorough analysis of its market trends, technological innovation, team members, and competition. This level of diligence will provide essential insights and inform better investment decisions.

The use of appropriate investment tools and platforms that offer advanced security and features tailored to cryptocurrency investing can help mitigate risk. These include cold storage wallets, two-factor authentication, and insurance policies for digital assets against theft or loss through the trading platform.

Developing the right mindset is imperative when dealing with cryptocurrencies. One must practice patience and avoid emotional trading. This means not giving in to fear during dips or becoming overly greedy when prices soar. Emotions can cloud judgment and lead to rash decisions that deviate from a well-thought-out strategy.

It's also wise to carefully consider the impact of taxes on your cryptocurrency investments. Understanding the tax obligations in your jurisdiction and incorporating tax planning into your investment strategy can help avoid unpleasant surprises and penalties from tax authorities.

Hedging is another strategy that investors can consider. This involves taking an offsetting position in a related asset to balance any potential losses. For example, if an investor holds a large position in a particular cryptocurrency, they can hedge by taking a short position in futures contracts for that cryptocurrency, thus balancing their exposure.

It's equally important to have an exit strategy in place. Before making any investment, decide on the conditions under which you would sell or reduce your positions. Defining these scenarios in advance helps in making objective decisions when the time comes.

Lastly, one of the best risk management practices is to maintain a balanced life perspective outside of investing. Having diverse interests and a stable personal life can act as a buffer against the highs and lows of the cryptocurrency market. It reinforces the understanding that investing in cryptocurrencies is just one part of a full and balanced life.

Remember, managing risk in cryptocurrency investing doesn't guarantee profits, but it does prepare you to navigate the market with a higher level of sophistication and composure. With careful planning, prudent strategies, and a disciplined approach, you can elevate your investing acumen and set a course for bright financial horizons.

In the next chapter, we'll delve into analyzing market trends, another key aspect of cryptocurrency investing that goes hand in hand with risk management. This will help you understand the ebbs and flows of the market, allowing for informed decision-making as you continue to grow and develop your investment portfolio.

Analyzing Market Trends

As we delve into the nuances of effectively analyzing market trends within the cryptocurrency landscape, it's imperative to comprehend how they can guide investment strategies. A well-versed investor observes the ebb and flow of the market with a blend of analytical tools and intuition developed through experience. This acumen is not innate but cultivated through consistent exposure and learning. Let's embark on this journey to decipher market trends and their potential impact on your investing decisions.

The paramount indicator of market trends is the price movement. Charts and graphs become the investor's canvas, portraying a visual representation of volatility, uptrends, and downturns. Concealed within these trends are patterns and indicators, such as moving averages or relative strength index (RSI), which aid in anticipating future movements. It's crucial to note that while historical data can shed light on potential outcomes, the cryptocurrency market's inherent volatility necessitates an agile approach. The ability to adapt to sudden changes can often make the difference between profit and peril.

A successful investor doesn't solely rely on technical analysis. Fundamental analysis also plays a pivotal role. This involves evaluating cryptocurrencies beyond price fluctuations, considering the broader economic picture. One must scrutinize market news, technological advancements, regulatory changes, and even the overall sentiment on social media and forums. Each of these factors can sway the market considerably, and astute investors integrate them into their analysis to garner a well-rounded view.

Understanding the impact of market sentiment is another key aspect of analyzing market trends. Sentiment can often drive the market more powerfully than any algorithm or statistic. Tools that measure the mood of the market, from fear and greed indexes to sentiment analysis algorithms, provide valuable insight into how the collective emotions of investors are likely to shape market behavior.

Volume, the amount of a cryptocurrency traded within a set period, also tells a story. An uptick in volume might precede a price increase, signaling a burgeoning interest, while a downturn may forecast a lack of confidence or a potential price decline. Pairing volume data with price trends can provide a stronger conviction about the veracity of a trend. Heavier volume means more significant attention and investment, which ideally translates into more stable trends.

Market capitalization, the total value of all coins in circulation, gives insight into the relative size and market share of different cryptocurrencies. Particularly when attempting to distinguish between established players and emerging contenders, market cap can be an insightful metric. It offers a frame of reference for the cryptocurrency's potential growth and sustainability.

Furthermore, liquidity metrics are crucial. Liquid markets allow for seamless entry and exit without substantial price impact. Assessing liquidity can help investors avoid the pitfalls of being trapped in positions due to thin trading volumes. Meanwhile, higher liquidity can indicate a mature market that is less susceptible to manipulation.

Correlation between cryptocurrencies is another point of study. Some coins and tokens tend to follow the price movements of market leaders like Bitcoin. These correlations can be exploited for strategic trades or to hedge against volatility. Understanding these relationships underpins a robust investment protocol by providing a mechanism to mitigate risk.

Emerging trends occasionally reshape the landscape. For instance, the adoption of decentralized finance (DeFi) has sparked new interest and market movements that defy traditional analysis. Investors are compelled to stay on the forefront of technology trends, such as DeFi, to leverage these waves as they rise.

Adopting a global perspective is also essential. Cryptocurrencies are not bound by national borders, and events around the world can ripple through the market. Markets may respond to policy changes in one country, technological advancements in another, and investment trends in a third. Cultivating an understanding of international developments allows investors to preempt and react to shifts catalyzed by global events.

Seasoned investors often use combinations of these tools to identify cyclical trends. Bullish and bearish cycles can extend over different time frames, and recognizing the phase of a cycle can influence trading strategies. For example, long-term holders might look past brief downtrends, while day traders capitalize on these short-term fluctuations.

Contrarian investors, who gauge when the market sentiment has reached extreme optimism or pessimism, can also benefit from understanding market trends. By positioning against the crowd when sentiment is too one-sided, they potentially reap rewards when the market corrects and sentiment shifts.

It's important to integrate various data points to evaluate the robustness of a trend. Drawing on diverse indicators helps to cross-verify signals and build confidence in one's investment decisions. An alignment across technical, fundamental, and sentiment indicators can herald the most reliable trends—a convergence that every vigilant investor seeks.

Finally, the risk of biases and emotional decision-making can be mitigated by a disciplined adherence to a pre-defined investment strategy. By systematically analyzing market trends and making informed decisions, investors minimize the impact of fear, greed, or FOMO (fear of missing out) on their actions.

Cultivating the skill to analyze market trends is an evolving process. It requires a balance of learning, experience, and adaptability. By carefully assessing price movements, market sentiment, volume, and other critical indicators, investors can make informed decisions that reap the benefits of this dynamic and revolutionary market. As with any journey, there's always more to learn, more territory to explore, and more potential to unlock. Take these insights as a starting point for a deeper exploration into the fascinating world of cryptocurrency market trends.

Portfolio Diversification Strategies

Intelligently mapping out a portfolio diversification plan is vital in taming the oft-times turbulent seas of cryptocurrency investment. Diversification is not simply a strategy; it's an art of balancing risk and potential rewards across various assets. It entails spreading investments to reduce risks related to individual crypto-assets. In this section, we'll delve into several strategies that can help you craft a resilient and growth-focused cryptocurrency portfolio.

The first principle in portfolio diversification involves understanding your risk tolerance. Risk is an inherent aspect of cryptocurrency due to market volatility. Before you diversify, assess how much risk you're willing to take. Younger investors might favor growth-oriented strategies with higher risk, while those closer to retirement might prioritize stability. It's essential to align your portfolio with your personal financial goals and risk appetite.

Secondly, when diversifying, consider the types of assets you're including. In cryptocurrency, this could mean distributing your investments across different coins and tokens. While Bitcoin might serve as a digital gold, altcoins like Ethereum or emergent tokens could present higher growth potential but carry more risk. It's not enough to invest across various assets; it's also prudent to seek out different value propositions and technological fundamentals.

Thirdly, engage with the idea of sector diversification. Just as you might diversify across industry sectors in a traditional stock portfolio, consider investing in cryptocurrencies that serve various sectors within the blockchain space. From finance-focused DeFi tokens to entertainment and media-oriented NFT platforms, each sector has its unique growth drivers and risks.

Fourth, pay attention to market cap diversification. Cryptocurrencies range from large-cap, established names to smaller, more speculative mid-cap and low-cap coins. Large-cap cryptos tend to be more stable, whereas smaller caps often present higher risk and potential for substantial returns. It's wise to have a mix, with a base of stability supplemented by opportunities for outsized gains.

Fifth, geographic diversification can also play a role in your strategy. Different countries have varying degrees of crypto acceptance and regulation, which can affect crypto assets based there. Diversifying across coins rooted in different legal jurisdictions can mitigate the risk of regulatory changes in any one country significantly impacting your portfolio.

Timely rebalancing is a crucial component of a diversification strategy. As the value of cryptocurrencies can change rapidly, so can the weight of your investments. Regularly adjusting your portfolio to maintain your desired allocation percentages can ensure that your risk level stays consistent with your goals.

Another divergent strategy is to delve into value and growth investing within the crypto space. Value coins or tokens may be those that are currently undervalued by the market but have strong fundamentals, while growth coins or tokens might be priced higher but have significant potential for market cap increase. Identifying and balancing between these can refine one's investment approach.

Building on this, layering in dividend or interest-bearing cryptocurrencies can enhance portfolio yields. Certain projects offer rewards or dividends for holding specific tokens, or you can earn interest through crypto staking or decentralized finance platforms. Including income-generating assets provides another vector of portfolio diversification.

It's also worth considering initial coin offerings (ICOs), security token offerings (STOs), or initial exchange offerings (IEOs) as they can offer early investment opportunities. However, these require due diligence as they can be especially risky and speculative. They should form only a small part of a well-diversified portfolio.

Moreover, investors shouldn't ignore the potential of automated diversification through the use of crypto index funds or ETFs. These financial instruments allow for investment across a broad range of assets within one vehicle, simplifying the diversification process and often lowering associated costs.

Nevertheless, remember the need for managing correlations within your portfolio. Cryptocurrencies can at times exhibit high correlation, moving similarly in response to market conditions. Seeking out non-correlated or inversely correlated assets helps ensure that not all your holdings move in the same direction at the same time.

It's also prudent to keep a global perspective and monitor the macroeconomic environment and its correlation with crypto markets. Diversifying across different asset classes, including traditional ones such as stocks, bonds, or commodities, can protect your crypto holdings from sector-specific downturns. This concept is known as cross-asset diversification.

Lastly, continuous education is a core element of successful diversification. The crypto market is dynamic, with new projects and technologies emerging regularly. Stay informed on the latest trends, advancements, and structural changes within the industry to refine your diversification approach.

In conclusion, portfolio diversification in the cryptocurrency world involves a blend of strategic asset allocation, sector consideration, attention to market cap, and nurturing a global, multi-class investment approach. Coupled with ongoing education and rebalancing, these strategies form the foundation of a robust investment framework designed to navigate the complexities of the cryptosphere. While there is no one-size-fits-all solution, a well-conceived diversification strategy is indispensable for any crypto investor looking to optimize their portfolio's risk-reward profile in pursuit of their financial objectives.

Chapter 6: Mining: Harvesting Digital Gold

Mining in the realm of cryptocurrency is akin to a modern-day gold rush, a process both exciting and intricate, acting as the backbone for many digital currencies. As we delve into the world of mining, we're exploring not just a method for creating new tokens, but also an essential mechanism for maintaining and securing blockchain networks. This chapter will illuminate the concept of mining, guiding you through the techniques that enable individuals and companies to harness computing power to validate transactions and, by extension, mint new digital coins—a process sometimes as elusive and alluring as the precious metals of old. From the electrical currents pulsating through high-powered hardware to the collective strength of mining pools, we unveil the strategic intricacies involved in becoming successful in this competitive endeavor. We're tapping into a world where patience, strategy, and technology intertwine, equipping you with the knowledge to understand the vein of digital wealth running through the cryptosphere. Embracing the complexity of mining ensures that your foray into the crypto universe is grounded in a strong comprehension of this pivotal activity.

How Mining Works

In the dynamic world of cryptocurrencies, mining stands at the core, fundamentally securing networks and minting new digital coins. Mining is no small endeavor; it's an industrial-grade operation that harnesses extensive computational power. This process is pivotal to the functioning of cryptocurrencies such as Bitcoin, which utilize a consensus mechanism termed Proof of Work (PoW). Let's embark on unraveling the intricate web that is cryptocurrency mining, step by step.

Mining is, at its heart, the act of solving complex mathematical problems. Miners use powerful computers to validate transactions on the cryptocurrency network. When transactions are made, they're grouped into a block. These blocks of transactions are not instantly certified. Instead, miners compete to verify the transactions by solving cryptographic puzzles that require tremendous computational effort.

The puzzles that are to be solved are essentially hashing problems. They require miners to produce a specific hash value that is less than or equal to the target hash set by the network. The target hash adjusts over time, maintaining the network's objective of producing a new block approximately every 10 minutes, at least in the case of Bitcoin.

The hashing process is exhaustive and random. Miners generate numerous hash combinations in rapid succession, hoping to find the 'golden nonce' – the one that solves the puzzle. It's akin to trying countless combinations to unlock a vault, where you can't predict which sequence will work, but when it does, the payoff is substantial.

Once the correct nonce is uncovered, the miner publishes the block to the network. The other nodes then verify the hash and if it checks out, the block is added to the blockchain. This block, now part of the ledger, represents a transparent, tamper-proof record of transactions.

The successful miner is rewarded for their efforts with a set number of new coins – this is known as the 'block reward'. The reward is an incentive mechanism, driving miners to contribute their computing power to the network. Notably, this block reward is halved periodically in an event called 'halving', reducing the rate at which new coins are generated.

In addition to the block reward, miners also receive transaction fees. These fees come from users who prioritize their transaction processing time by paying a premium. As the block reward continues to halve over time, these transaction fees are meant to become a more significant part of a miner's income.

The competition among miners is fierce, and only the first to solve the puzzle receives the reward. This induces an arms race in mining technology – miners continually seek more powerful and energy-efficient hardware to stay ahead. It's a round-the-clock operation with heavy energy consumption, prompting a critical examination of the environmental impact of cryptocurrency mining.

Decentralization is a foundational aspect of cryptocurrency, and mining contributes to this property. By spreading the mining operations across a global network, it becomes nearly impossible for any single entity to corrupt the entire system. Miners are the sentinels of the blockchain, ensuring its security and integrity.

Proof of Work, while robust, is not without its drawbacks. The intensive energy use and the fact that the rewards favor those with more significant computational resources pinpoint the issues at the center of discussions about mining's future. This has led to the exploration of alternative consensus mechanisms like Proof of Stake (PoS) that aim to be more energy-efficient and equitable, but those are discussions for another section.

Over time, individual miners have seen their ability to compete diminish as mining turned into a more industrial operation, with companies investing in vast mining farms. These farms are filled with specialized hardware like Application Specific Integrated Circuits (ASICs) designed solely for mining cryptocurrencies, offering a performance and energy consumption that general-purpose hardware can't match.

Mining pools have emerged as a response to the increasing difficulty of mining solo. These pools allow individual miners to collaborate, combining their computational power to compete more effectively. When the pool succeeds in mining a block, the reward is shared among its participants relative to the amount of computational work they contributed.

As cryptocurrencies continue to evolve, the role of miners does too. Emerging technologies and changes in consensus mechanisms may significantly change the mining landscape. For now, mining remains an essential function of many cryptocurrency networks, providing security and minting new coins in what has become a digital age gold rush.

The world of mining is an integral part of the cryptocurrency ecosystem. Its complexities are many, its impact on the viability and security of digital currencies is immense, and its evolution is certain. As an aspiring developer, entrepreneur, or investor, understanding this foundation is critical. While mining may be an energy-intensive game of chance and expertise, its role in the underpinnings of digital currency is unquestionable.

Thus, as we look toward the future of cryptocurrencies, the act of mining remains central to many digital currencies. It serves as a reminder of the sheer power of decentralization, and the relentless innovation that underpins one of the most fascinating technological revolutions of our time.

Choosing Hardware for Mining

Mining cryptocurrency is akin to entering a competitive lottery where success hinges on speed, efficiency, and strategic investment. The selection of mining hardware is a fundamental decision, determining the potential return on investment, overall expenses, and mining capability. The process of finding the perfect configuration can be daunting; however, with a methodical approach, one can navigate these waters with informed confidence.

Initially, understanding the two primary types of mining hardware – ASICs and GPUs – is crucial. ASICs, or Application-Specific Integrated Circuits, are devices specifically designed for mining certain cryptocurrencies, offering unparalleled efficiency for their designated coin. However, their use is limited only to one or a few similar types of algorithms. Conversely, GPUs, or Graphics Processing Units, are versatile, enabling miners to switch between different cryptocurrencies and adapt to changing market conditions, albeit at a lower efficiency than their ASIC counterparts.

Evaluating the cost of hardware is an imperative factor in the decision-making process. It's not merely the initial expenditure that must be considered but also the operational costs, including electricity consumption. High-performing machines often require more power, which can significantly increase ongoing costs. Miners must assess their local electricity rates and the power draw of potential hardware to ensure a sustainable mining operation.

Actionably, scrutinizing the hashrate, which measures the computational power of the mining device, is essential. The higher the hashrate, the greater the number of calculations the hardware can perform, increasing the likelihood of successful mining block rewards. Nevertheless, a balance between hashrate and power consumption is key since a high hashrate with disproportionate power usage may not yield the most profitable outcome.

Mining hardware's durability and build quality also merit attention. Given that mining machinery operates around the clock, durable components can reduce the frequency of repairs or replacements. Reliability ensures a steady mining process, which is critical because downtime equates to missed opportunities for earning cryptocurrency rewards.

While looking at hardware specifications, one must also consider the noise and heat output. Mining equipment can produce significant noise levels, which may be problematic for residential settings. Moreover, effective heat dissipation is paramount to preserve the longevity of the hardware, requiring miners to implement adequate cooling solutions, which may add to the overall cost.

It's also critical to recognize the potential resale value of the mining equipment. ASIC miners may lose value rapidly if a new, more efficient model is released or if the cryptocurrency they target loses popularity. GPUs generally retain value better, as they can be repurposed for gaming or other computing tasks. This residual value can serve as a form of risk mitigation should a miner decide to exit the mining space.

Considering network difficulty is another essential aspect of the hardware selection process. As more miners join the network, the difficulty of mining increases, which can reduce the profitability of older or less powerful hardware. This dynamic ecosystem necessitates forward-thinking and often a readiness to upgrade to more advanced equipment to stay competitive in the mining game.

Brand reputation and customer service offered by hardware manufacturers should not be overlooked. Well-established companies typically provide better support and warranties, which can be invaluable when addressing technical issues or hardware failures. Long-term service safeguarding your investment can prove invaluable, especially in an industry where every minute of downtime can result in lost revenue.

Now, because cryptocurrency mining is an arms race of sorts, considering future-proofing one's investment makes perfect sense. It is wise to invest in hardware that not only meets current mining demands but also has the potential to remain competitive for a reasonable period. This prescience can lead to better sustainability of mining operations as the network evolves.

Moreover, compatibility with mining pools and software is a factor that should not be sidestepped. Certain mining pools might only support specific types of hardware or software configurations. Ensuring your mining setup aligns with the requirements of your chosen mining pool is essential for a seamless integration.

When it comes to the environmental impact, choosing hardware with a lower carbon footprint can be not only a socially responsible decision but can also confer a competitive edge as scrutiny on energy consumption intensifies within the industry.

In addition to the hardware's direct features and qualifications, availability of the equipment matters as well. High demand can lead to stock shortages, delays in delivery, and even price inflation. Staying updated on market trends, pre-ordering units, or even seeking second-hand hardware can be strategies to overcome these potential obstacles.

Last, but certainly not least, educating oneself through community forums, product reviews, and tutorials is an enduring piece of advice. Engage with other miners and industry experts to garner insightful perspectives. This collective knowledge can illuminate aspects of mining hardware you might not have previously considered and direct you toward a more suitable choice.

In conclusion, choosing the right hardware for mining is a multifaceted process that requires a holistic approach. From calculating costs and potential profits to considering operational nuances and future market conditions, each element plays a pivotal role in the success of a cryptocurrency mining venture. With a strategic and informed selection, miners can optimize their operations for long-term profitability and sustainability.

Joining a Mining Pool

In the realm of cryptocurrency mining, joining a mining pool is akin to combining resources in a collective—an endeavor that can significantly increase the odds of reaping rewards in the digital gold landscape. For individuals aiming to mine cryptocurrency, understanding mining pools is crucial. This section will serve as a practical roadmap for connecting with a pool and harmonize your mining journey with the efforts of others.

At its core, a mining pool is a network of miners who contribute their computing power to increase the probability of successfully mining a block. The complexities of mining, especially for currencies like Bitcoin, are such that solo efforts can prove to be inefficient and rarely rewarding for individual miners. A mining pool, therefore, is an answer to the mounting difficulty levels that solo miners face.

To begin, you must select a mining pool that aligns with your needs and values. Factors to consider include the pool's size, the fees they charge, the frequency of payouts, the geographic location of their servers, and the consensus mechanism they operate under. A larger pool might offer more regular payouts, but often these come with higher fees and potentially smaller reward shares. Conversely, a smaller pool might offer larger reward shares but at the risk of less frequent payouts.

Once you've selected your preferred pool, the next step is to register as a member. This process typically involves creating an account on the pool's website. Registration usually requires providing an email address, setting up a username, and choosing a secure password. Some pools might also require a two-factor authentication setup to enhance security.

After registering, you will need to set up your mining hardware. This involves configuring your mining devices with the specific details provided by your mining pool. Details include the pool's server address, port number, your username, and worker identifier. Often, pools provide detailed instructions or even pre-configured files to simplify this process.

Configuration is essential, as it ensures that any cryptocurrency you mine is attributed to your account. Be meticulous during this process, as any mistake can lead to mining effort being lost or credited to another miner. Thankfully, most mining pools offer customer support avenues to assist with any configuration difficulties.

When your mining hardware is up and running, you'll begin contributing to the pool's collective hashing power. As a collective, the pool works to solve complex cryptographic puzzles which, when solved, result in the creation of a new block on the blockchain. These efforts, when successful, are rewarded with cryptocurrency.

The rewards from mining activities are then distributed among the pool members. Distribution is based on the amount of work, often referred to as shares, that each miner has contributed. Remember that fees will be subtracted from your rewards, so you should always be aware of the fee structure your pool has in place.

Monitoring your mining operation is vital. Most pools offer dashboards that provide real-time statistics about your mining activity, such as hashrate, total shares submitted, and estimated earnings. This feedback allows you to make informed decisions about your mining strategy and troubleshoot any problems that may arise.

It's vital to note that no mining pool can guarantee profits. The fluctuating nature of cryptocurrency value, increasing mining difficulty, and operational costs such as electricity can all impact your profitability. Being part of a pool does facilitate a more predictable mining outcome, but it's not without its risks and variable factors.

Security is another critical aspect you must not overlook when joining a mining pool. Ensure that the pool has a robust security framework in place to protect its miners. This includes secure connections to the pool servers and regular payouts to your wallet to minimize potential losses from pool wallet breaches.

In addition to security, communication within the pool community can be beneficial. Engaging with other miners in forums or chat groups can provide insights, allow the sharing of tips, and grant a better overall mining experience. Such communities reinforce the educational and collaborative spirit of the cryptocurrency world.

As you mine, keeping abreast of changes in the pool's policies and the broader cryptocurrency market is strategic. Pools can change fee structures, payout methods, or other operations which may directly affect your mining profitability. Staying informed will also help you anticipate shifts in consensus mechanisms or algorithm updates which may necessitate changes in your mining hardware or software configurations.

Lastly, don't forget to consider the tax implications of your mining efforts. In many jurisdictions, revenue from mining is considered taxable income, and you must report it accordingly. Depending on the structure of the pool, they may or may not provide tax-related documenttation, so it's crucial to keep your records meticulously.

In conclusion, joining a mining pool may significantly improve your chances of success in the cryptocurrency mining venture. By following the steps outlined and staying informed, you can streamline your participation and optimize your potential rewards. As you integrate into the pool community and contribute your processing power, remember that every miner plays a critical part in the decentralized future of finance.

While the digital gold rush landscape is ever-changing, with new technologies and regulations constantly emerging, being part of a mining pool aligns you closely with the pulse of this dynamic industry. Your decision to mine within a collective is not merely a strategic move for personal gain but a harmonious contribution to the robustness and security of the blockchain network. This collaborative spirit is the keystone of cryptocurrency's enduring strength and revolutionary potential.

Chapter 7: Navigating the Regulatory Landscape

As we pivot from the mechanics and strategies around mining digital gold, we enter a maze tinged with legalese and jurisdictional quirks: the regulatory landscape. The trailblazing nature of cryptocurrencies means that laws are often racing to keep up, presenting a multi-faceted puzzle for participants. This chapter serves as a map to traverse this complex terrain, illuminating the reader on the necessity of understanding legal frameworks that govern the space. Without a grasp of regulations, one runs the risk of unintentional missteps with potentially serious consequences. We'll explore why knowing your customer (KYC) and anti-money laundering (AML) requirements aren't just buzzwords but essential compliances for maintaining the integrity of your ventures. As global regulations—often as variable as the value of the currencies themselves—continue to transform, staying informed isn't just best practice, it's imperative for survival and success in this evolving digital economy. We articulate this not just to alarm but to empower; with knowledge comes the confidence to navigate the legalities that encapsulate the vibrant world of cryptocurrencies.

Legal Implications of Cryptocurrencies

The emergence of cryptocurrencies as a novel financial asset class has not just revolutionized the way we perceive money but has also caught the attention of various regulatory bodies. While some have lauded cryptocurrencies for their potential to democratize finance, others have expressed concerns over their potential to sidestep traditional financial regulations.

One of the foremost legal considerations concerning cryptocurrencies is their classification. The debate rages on whether they should be treated as a currency, a commodity, or a security, with different countries taking different stances. This classification affects how cryptocurrencies are regulated, taxed, and legally recognized.

In the United States, for example, the Internal Revenue Service (IRS) treats cryptocurrencies as property for tax purposes, meaning transactions involving cryptocurrency are subject to capital gains tax. However, the Securities and Exchange Commission (SEC) has, at times, considered them as securities, particularly when it comes to Initial Coin Offerings (ICOs), thus subjecting them to a different regulatory framework.

Moreover, the use of cryptocurrencies in illicit activities has drawn significant scrutiny from governments worldwide. The pseudo-anonymous nature of cryptocurrency transactions makes them an attractive means for money laundering, terrorist financing, and other criminal enterprises. This has led to a push for more stringent Anti-Money Laundering (AML) and Know Your Customer (KYC) laws in the sector, with many exchanges now required to perform identity checks and report suspicious activities.

Cross-border transactions with cryptocurrencies can further complicate the legal landscape. Global regulatory standards remain non-uniform, thus making international operations in the crypto-sphere a complex legal challenge for businesses and individuals alike. Global bodies like the Financial Action Task Force (FATF) have been working to create a set of guidelines that member countries can adapt to regulate cryptocurrencies and service providers in this space.

The deployment of smart contracts on blockchain platforms raises yet another set of legal issues. Smart contracts are self-executing contracts with the terms directly written into code. While this technology offers the potential for trustless agreements without intermediaries, it also begs the question of legal enforceability and jurisdiction, especially when disputes arise.

The decentralized nature of many cryptocurrencies also raises concerns about consumer protection. Without a central authority or a traditional legal framework applicable, users may have limited recourse in disputes, fraud, or theft. Additionally, the rapid evolution of the technology can outpace legal systems, leading to grey areas in consumer protection laws.

Initial Coin Offerings (ICOs), once a popular means of fundraising for new cryptocurrency projects, have faced significant legal challenges, too. The lack of regulation around ICOs led to a proliferation of scams and fraudulent schemes, ultimately catalyzing regulatory bodies to step in and take action to protect investors.

Asset inheritance is yet another domain where traditional legal systems encounter challenges with cryptocurrencies. The private keys required to access and transfer cryptocurrencies highlight the need for careful estate planning and raise issues about the transfer of digital assets after death, a topic that many jurisdictions are still grappling with.

The integration of cryptocurrencies with traditional financial services and products, such as banks offering custody services, brings these assets further under the purview of existing financial regulations. As institutional investors enter the space, compliance with regulations traditionally associated with securities and investment products becomes critical.

Privacy coins, which provide enhanced anonymity features, challenge the present legal frameworks centered around financial transparency. Regulators often perceive these coins as a tool to conceal financial dealings, leading some jurisdictions to consider banning their use altogether.

Looking at intellectual property rights, the open-source nature of many blockchain projects juxtaposed against the proprietary technologies developed by various firms introduces a complex matrix of legal considerations related to patent law, copyright, and trademark issues.

Environmental regulations have also come to the fore as large-scale cryptocurrency mining consumes tremendous amounts of power, prompting some governments to scrutinize the environmental impact of such operations and consider regulatory measures to control carbon footprints.

Lastly, as litigation involving cryptocurrencies becomes more prevalent, the legal profession itself must adapt and develop expertise in this emerging field. This includes understanding technical details of blockchain technology as well as the evolving landscape of regulations and case law.

Navigating the regulatory landscape of cryptocurrencies requires vigilance and adaptability. Entities engaged in cryptocurrency transactions must stay informed of local and global regulatory developments to mitigate legal risks. As the space matures, one can expect a more robust and comprehensive legal framework to evolve, offering greater clarity and protection for all participants in this revolutionary financial ecosystem.

KYC and AML in the Crypto World

In the burgeoning landscape of digital currencies, understanding the role of Know Your Customer (KYC) and Anti-Money Laundering (AML) regulations is pivotal. These protocols, though sometimes seen as antithetical to the core philosophies of privacy and decentralization that many cryptocurrencies were built upon, play a critical role in maintaining the legitimacy and stability of the crypto space. They serve as a bridge between the relatively unregulated world of crypto-currencies and the stringent demands of global financial law.

Starting with KYC, an acronym for Know Your Customer (or Know Your Client), these regulations require financial institutions to verify the identity of their clients. In the realm of cryptocurrency, this typically involves a process where users must submit personal identification documents when they register for an exchange or a wallet service. This is not only to establish the user's identity but also to create a foundation of trust and transparency within the ecosystem.

AML regulations, on the other hand, are designed to prevent money laundering activities. These rules ensure that platforms observe patterns that might suggest financial transactions are being used to launder money, support terrorism, or engage in other illegal activities. Crypto exchanges, for example, must report suspicious activities to authorities and take steps to minimize the risk of facilitating criminal behavior.

One might wonder why there's a need for KYC and AML in an environment that values anonymity. The truth is, while anonymity provides users with privacy, it can also make cryptocurrency a haven for illicit activities. To counteract this, regulators worldwide have been enforcing KYC and AML requirements with increasing strictness, aiming to bring cryptocurrency transactions into the light without fully compromising user privacy.

The process of adhering to these regulations starts with understanding them. Businesses operating within the crypto space must be well-versed in the specific requirements of the jurisdictions in which they operate. Not all countries have the same rules, and what may be sufficient in one country may be lacking in another. This patchwork regulatory environment adds a layer of complexity for crypto-related businesses which must navigate varying international laws.

Although it might seem burdensome, compliance with KYC and AML standards can offer legitimate benefits to users. For one, it helps protect investors by ensuring that the platforms they are using are taking steps to prevent fraudulent activities. This can bring a sense of security and help stabilize the overall ecosystem by creating a more reliable and trustworthy environment for trading and investment.

Furthermore, institutional investors, who have the potential to inject significant capital into the market, often require a level of regulatory certainty before they will engage. Thus, the adoption of KYC and AML standards by crypto platforms can attract these traditional investors, providing a boon to the market's growth and maturity.

Implementing KYC and AML measures can be a challenge for crypto businesses. It requires a delicate balance of respecting user privacy and maintaining an open platform, while also deterring financial crimes. Crypto platforms often employ a range of technologies, such as biometric verification and AI-powered transaction monitoring systems, to meet these dual objectives.

One of the key concerns is the centralization of data that KYC processes can create. Submitting personal identification to various platforms creates multiple points of vulnerability where user information could potentially be accessed by unauthorized parties. Consequently, this has sparked interest in developing solutions such as decentralized identity verification systems that could allow users to prove their identity without overexposing personal information.

The approach to AML in the crypto world also necessitates a robust analysis of transaction patterns. Advanced algorithms and analytical tools are crucial in identifying potential red flags, which can then be investigated manually. This combination of automated tools and human oversight forms the frontline in the battle against illegal activities within the crypto space.

There are also continuing debates about how KYC and AML requirements affect the broader goals of cryptocurrencies. While some argue that such measures are essential, others believe they undermine the original intent of digital currencies to provide a level of autonomy and privacy not available in traditional finance. Regardless of one's stance, it is clear these regulations are here to stay and must be effectively managed.

Indeed, regulatory clarity can serve as a framework for innovation. By establishing clear rules and expectations, developers and entrepreneurs can focus on building new products and services within a known legal context. This can lead to the development of safer and more consumer-friendly cryptocurrency services, while still harnessing the transformative power of the blockchain technology.

Navigating KYC and AML requirements in the crypto world isn't just about compliance; it's also about embracing the evolving intersection of technology, finance, and law. As the cryptocurrency market continues to grow and mature, these regulations may also evolve, reflecting a dynamic relationship between innovation and the need for a stable, predictable financial system.

To sum up, KYC and AML frameworks serve as integral checkpoints in the digital economy, aiming to legitimize and stabilize the cryptocurrency marketplace. By requiring identity verification and monitoring suspicious activities, crypto businesses can be part of a broader effort to deter financial crimes while fostering trust and attracting investment. As participants in the crypto realm, it's our shared responsibility to champion the mechanisms that support its integrity, ensuring a sustainable future for digital currencies.

As you continue your journey through the vast realms of cryptocurrency and blockchain, remember that understanding regulations, such as KYC and AML, is as much a part of digital asset literacy as knowing about blockchain forks or smart contract vulnerabilities. In the subsequent chapters, we will look further into other layers of the regulatory landscape and their impact on global economies, keeping a keen eye on how these dynamics shape the future of money and innovation.

Global Regulations and Their Impact

As the world continues to wrestle with the technological tidal wave that is cryptocurrencies, a patchwork of global regulations has emerged, shaping the evolution and adoption of digital assets. The impact of these regulations is far-reaching, affecting not only investors and developers but also the very essence of how cryptocurrencies operate. Understanding the global regulatory landscape is crucial for anyone involved in the crypto space, whether you're making your first investment or developing a new digital asset.

At their core, cryptocurrencies promise a decentralized future, where financial transactions are not governed by central authorities. However, the reality is more complex, as regulatory bodies around the world have started to impose rules to control this newfound digital realm. The rationale behind such regulations often stems from a need to protect investors, prevent money laundering, and maintain the integrity of financial markets.

In the United States, for example, the Securities and Exchange Commission (SEC) has become increasingly vocal about its stance on digital assets, treating many of them as securities. This classification brings a myriad of compliance requirements for both issuers of initial coin offerings (ICOs) and exchanges that list these digital assets. The implications are profound, as startups and established companies alike must navigate the intricate legal landscape to avoid penalties and legal battles.

Across the Atlantic, the European Union has been crafting its own set of regulations, keen on fostering innovation while safeguarding stakeholders. The General Data Protection Regulation (GDPR), although not exclusively targeting cryptocurrencies, has significant repercussions for blockchain technologies, demanding greater privacy and data protection. Meanwhile, the EU's Fifth Anti-Money Laundering Directive (5AMLD) extends its reach to cover crypto exchanges and wallet providers, requiring stricter identity checks.

In Asia, regulatory approaches vary significantly. Countries like Japan have embraced digital currencies, creating a regulatory framework that provides clarity and security for users and businesses. On the other hand, China has taken a much more restrictive stance, outright banning ICOs and cracking down on all cryptocurrency trading within its borders. This diverse regulatory environment reflects the ongoing global debate regarding the role of cryptocurrencies in the financial system.

Such disparate regulatory responses across countries have inspired both innovation and caution within the crypto community. Complex legal structures are being created by crypto businesses to comply with varying regulations, while some have moved their operations to more crypto-friendly jurisdictions, a phenomenon known as regulatory arbitrage.

For investors, the implications of global regulations are twofold. Firstly, there's a need for heightened diligence; with regulations continually evolving, staying informed is paramount to ensuring compliance and protecting one's investments. Secondly, regulations can influence market dynamics. A favorable regulatory announcement may lead to a surge in market confidence, while an unfavorable one can trigger a swift downturn.

From the perspective of innovation, regulations can both hinder and foster growth. Strict rules may dampen creativity and dissuade new entrants, while clear and fair regulations can provide a stable environment that encourages innovation. Projects that may have thrived in a decentralized, unfettered ecosystem might find themselves having to adapt to these regulations or risk becoming irrelevant.

Regulatory bodies also grapple with how to tax cryptocurrencies, which remains a complex issue due to the borderless nature of digital assets and the technological mechanisms behind them. Users are often unsure about their tax obligations, and governments are challenged to track and enforce these due to the pseudonymous nature of transactions.

Another significant impact of regulation is on the technology itself. Certain features and functions of blockchain might need to be tweaked or redesigned to comply with regulations. For example, the immutable nature of blockchain could be at odds with laws that require the ability to erase personal information. Developers are hence incentivized to create privacy-oriented solutions that can still comply with such regulations without sacrificing the core principles of blockchain technology.

Moreover, regulations affect the global competitiveness of nations. Countries that create early, clear, and innovative regulatory frameworks may attract more crypto-related businesses, positioning themselves as leaders in the future financial ecosystem. Alternatively, countries with ambiguous or restrictive regulations may find themselves left behind.

The challenge for regulators worldwide is to strike the right balance between innovation and consumer protection. This requires a nuanced understanding of both the technology and the unique attributes of digital assets. It's an ongoing process that seeks to reconcile the fast pace of technological advancements with a legal system that often moves at a slower cadence.

One promising development in the regulatory space is the emerging discussion around "regulatory sandboxes." These are frameworks set up by regulatory bodies that allow fintech and crypto startups to test out new products and services within a controlled environment, without immediately having to comply with all the existing financial regulations.

Finally, transnational collaborations, like the Financial Action Task Force (FATF), are working towards harmonizing regulations across borders to ensure a more consistent approach to cryptocurrency and reduce the potential for regulatory arbitrage. These organizations are pivotal in shaping regulations that consider both international standards and local nuances.

In conclusion, as the cryptocurrency landscape continues to mature, so too must the regulatory frameworks that govern it. The interplay between regulation and digital assets remains a critical narrative influencing the growth, innovation, and adoption of this burgeoning asset class. For the engaged observer, entrepreneur, or investor, staying vigilant and well-informed on these regulatory winds is not just advisable; it's essential to the intelligent navigation of the crypto sphere.

Chapter 8: Security and Safety in the Cryptosphere

Venturing further into the cryptosphere, we realize that beyond the allure of innovation and potential profits, there's a critical need for vigilance and robust security measures. In Chapter 8, we delve into the best practices to safeguard your digital assets, emphasizing the significance of choosing reliable hardware wallets and secure password protocols. The conversation steers towards the strategies experts use to identify and mitigate risks, including recognizing the red flags that signal scams in their many guises. Ciphering through encryption and cybersecurity introduces a layer of technical defense that protects transactions and storage of cryptocurrency funds. It's not just about understanding the threats, but equipping ourselves with the knowledge to preemptively counter them, ensuring that we become active participants in our financial security within the ever-evolving cryptosphere.

Protecting Your Investments

When entering the realm of cryptocurrency, the concept of security takes on a profoundly important role. As we've seen in previous chapters, the crypto world is fraught with its own unique set of risks and challenges. In this section, we'll explore practical steps and sophisticated strategies to safeguard your investments in this volatile and often unpredictable market.

First and foremost, the cornerstone of protecting your digital assets is understanding the importance of a secure wallet. Whether you opt for a hardware wallet, which stores cryptocurrencies offline and is considered one of the safest options, or a software wallet that offers convenience and quicker access, the key is to choose a wallet from a reputable provider with robust security measures. Always remember, your private keys are the lifeline to your investments; keep them secret and keep them safe.

Two-factor authentication (2FA) is another layer of security you can't afford to overlook. This step requires not only something you know, such as a password or PIN, but also something you have, like a mobile device or 2FA fob. Activating 2FA on every exchange account and related service can dramatically reduce the risk of unauthorized access. It's a simple process that adds a significant security upgrade.

Phishing scams are prevalent, and the crypto community is a prime target. Be highly cautious with the emails and messages you receive, especially those that request your credentials or private information. Verify the authenticity of websites before entering sensitive data, and consider bookmarking the legitimate sites you frequently use. Awareness and skepticism online are your best defenses against these deceptive practices.

Given that exchanges are a central aspect of cryptocurrency trading and can be hotbeds for hacking attempts, it's prudent to use them only for trades. Avoid storing large sums of cryptocurrency on an exchange. Instead, transfer funds to and from your personal wallet when trading. Not only does this reduce your exposure on these platforms, but it also puts you in complete control of your assets, which is the essence of cryptocurrency's empowering potential.

Diversification is not just a strategy for investment portfolios—it's also a strategic approach to security. By spreading your assets across different wallets, exchanges, and even storage mediums, you mitigate the risk that any one security breach could wipe out your investments. With an array of baskets, even if one falls, not all your eggs are broken.

An often underestimated yet incredibly effective protective measure is maintaining up-to-date antivirus and antimalware software. Cyber threats are constantly evolving, and your digital defense should be, too. Make sure all devices used for cryptocurrency transactions are protected with the latest cybersecurity solutions. Regular software updates are equally essential, as they often include patches for known vulnerabilities.

Backing up your wallet can save you from a host of troubles, including technical failures and human error. Keep multiple backups in different secure locations. This could mean having physical copies in the form of paper wallets or hardware wallet backups, as well as encrypted digital backups stored on separate, offline devices. In the event of data loss, these backups will be your retrieval roadmap.

It's worth noting that not all cryptocurrencies are created equal when it comes to security features. Some have built-in privacy features such as stealth addresses and ring signatures, while others prioritize transparency. It's important to understand the inherent security features of the cryptocurrencies you choose to invest in and how they align with your investment strategy.

When it comes to communication about your investments, discretion should be your watchword. The less people know about your holdings, the better. Unfortunately, social engineering attacks are a reality and can range from simple online requests to elaborate offline contrivances designed to extract sensitive information from you. Keep your investment details and strategies to yourself, barring professional advice from a trusted financial advisor.

Setting up a separate email address that you use solely for cryptocurrency transactions can further streamline your security practices. This email should not be tied to any personal or professional activities, thereby limiting potential attack vectors. It becomes the dedicated communication channel for your exchanges, wallets, and crypto-related interactions.

Using secure and private internet connections is also fundamental in protecting your investments. Public Wi-Fi networks, for example, are notoriously insecure, making them a bad choice for trading or managing your digital assets. Stick to trusted networks, preferably your own, and consider the use of a reputable Virtual Private Network (VPN) when conducting transactions to mask your IP address and online footprint.

Legal protections should not be ignored, whether it's in the form of insurance offered by an exchange or a personal asset protection strategy. As much as possible, utilize the services of platforms that provide some level of indemnity against loss due to operational issues or security breaches. Be aware, though, that in the current climate, such protections may be limited and can vary significantly between services.

Smart contracts, a key feature highlighted in earlier chapters, can be a tool for investment protection when applied correctly. They provide automated, immutable agreements that offer assurance transactions will execute only as described without interference. However, it's vital to understand that the code of a smart contract is only as good as its programming, so due diligence is paramount before entering into such agreements.

For those who engage in frequent trading, using trading bots may provide benefits like speed and efficiency, but they should be employed with caution. Not only must the security of such bots be considered, but traders should be conversant with their operational parameters to avoid unintended trades that can lead to substantial losses. Knowledge and oversight are essential components when incorporating any automated systems into your trading strategy.

Last but not least, education is the bedrock upon which all other investment protection measures rest. An informed investor is a secure investor. Keep abreast of the latest developments in cryptocurrency security, familiarize yourself with new threats, and stay engaged with the community. The more you know, the better prepared you'll be when it comes to defending your financial future in the cryptosphere.

With these strategies and precautions in place, you can turn your focus toward the vast opportunities that cryptocurrencies provide with greater confidence and peace of mind. The digital landscape is ever-changing, progressing—and so should our approaches to safeguarding our hard-earned assets within it. Secure your knowledge, and your investments will follow.

Mitigating Risks and Recognizing Scams

When delving into the cryptocurrency sphere, one should be ever-vigilant to protect against the twin dangers of risks and scams. Both can swiftly sever the ties between an investor and their investment, often with no chance of recovery. Therefore, it's critical to have a strategic approach to mitigation that is composed of awareness, education, and practical actions.

Understanding the risks inherent in cryptocurrency investment starts with the volatile nature of digital currencies. While immense gains are possible, so too are crushing losses. To mitigate against market volatility, it's important to never invest more than you can afford to lose. Approach investment with a clear strategy, set stop-loss orders to limit potential losses, and regularly review your investment portfolio to adjust to changing market conditions.

Scams in the cryptocurrency world manifest in various forms, such as phishing attempts, fake ICOs, or Ponzi schemes. To steer clear of such deceits, always conduct thorough research before investing. Be skeptical of promises which seem too good to be true — they often are.

Verify the credentials of any company or individual and seek out independent analysis and reviews of any investment opportunity.

Another key component of risk mitigation is due diligence. When participating in an ICO or buying tokens, deep-dive into the project's whitepaper, understand the use case, check the project's code if available, and scrutinize the team's background. Legitimacy is often substantiated by transparency: if details are obscured or responses to queries are unsatisfactory, exercise caution.

Cybersecurity threats are rampant in the cryptosphere. Protecting your digital assets involves using secure passwords, enabling two-factor authentication, and using hardware wallets for storing crypto-currencies. Keep your devices updated with the latest security software, and be wary of unsolicited communications or dubious links that could lead to phishing sites.

Social media platforms are breeding grounds for crypto-scams. Be wary of supposed "investment gurus" or social media profiles that promise quick returns or insider tips in exchange for sending cryptocurrency. These are often fronts for fraud. Use social media judiciously, seeking information but always cross-referencing any advice with reputable sources.

Understanding common scam setups can also help in recognizing and avoiding them. For instance, 'pump and dump' schemes involve artificially inflating the price of a currency before selling it off at a profit to the detriment of other investors. Being aware of these schemes allows you to spot unnatural patterns in cryptocurrency movements that may indicate manipulative activities.

Education is a potent tool against risks and scams. Participating in online forums, attending webinars, and taking courses can increase your knowledge and ability to spot red flags. Moreover, connecting with a community of cryptocurrency enthusiasts provides a platform for sharing experiences and staying informed about emerging threats.

Government and regulatory bodies are increasing their oversight of the cryptocurrency market. Staying informed about up-to-date regulations helps you to remain compliant and to identify illegitimate operations that might be bypassing legal requirements. Regulations are not just obstacles; they can be signposts for secure investment routes.

Risk mitigation in cryptocurrency also includes recognition of the technology's limitations. Understanding the mechanics of blockchain, the finality of transactions, and the absence of chargebacks in cryptocurrency transactions helps you to grasp the importance of precision in your dealings. Mistakes can be irreversible, so ensuring accuracy in all transactions is necessary.

Building a diversified portfolio can help in spreading risk. Don't place all your digital eggs in one cryptocurrency basket. Spread your investments across different assets, which might include not only various cryptocurrencies but traditional investments too. That way, should one aspect of the portfolio underperform, the impact upon your overall investments might be mitigated.

Lastly, continue to educate yourself. The cryptocurrency landscape is perpetually evolving, with new risks and scams arising as technologies advance and proliferate. Keeping abreast of these developments is not a one-time endeavor, but a continuous journey. Regularly update your knowledge to safeguard your investments.

When it comes to recognizing and avoiding scams, intuition should not be underestimated. If an opportunity triggers your sense of skepticism or seems out of place, take a step back and reassess. Often, a gut feeling can save you from becoming ensnared in a scammer's net. Remember, if in doubt, it's better to err on the side of caution than to fall victim to fraud.

It's also important to maintain perspective and not be led by emotion. FOMO (fear of missing out) can lead investors to make hasty, ill-considered decisions, which scammers can exploit. Take your time with decisions, allowing yourself a clear head to think through potential investments.

In conclusion, mitigating risk and recognizing scams in the cryptocurrency arena requires a blend of knowledge, vigilance, and common sense. Educating yourself, staying current with market developments, leveraging technology for security, and connecting with a network of fellow investors are all critical tools in your arsenal to protect your digital assets. As the adage goes, forewarned is forearmed, and in the ever-shifting landscape of cryptocurrency, this has never been more true.

The Role of Encryption and Cybersecurity

As we've delved into the intricacies of cryptocurrency and blockchain, we've uncovered a digital ecosystem where security is not just advisable; it's an absolute necessity. In this nurturing environment for digital assets, encryption and cybersecurity emerge as pivotal elements. The sanctity of digital transactions and the storage of cryptographic currencies depend heavily on a robust cybersecurity framework. Let's unpack these concepts and understand their place in the crypto world.

Encryption is the cornerstone of cryptocurrency's security. It's a process that transforms readable data into a cipher or code to prevent unauthorized access. The privilege of being able to execute transactions on blockchain platforms is predicated on the possession of private keys—strings of cryptographic information that are, in essence, the embodiment of a user's ownership and access rights. These keys are encrypted; compromising them would be akin to handing over the keys to one's digital kingdom.

But encryption is more dynamic than a static guard. It's the hallmark of blockchain technology and shapes everything from a user's wallet to each transaction's integrity that's ever been inscribed on the blockchain. It helps ensure that 'digital gold'—be it Bitcoin, Ethereum, or any altcoins—remains secure yet transferrable in a trustless environment.

Cybersecurity, while inclusive of encryption, spans a broader aspect. It's about implementing a spectrum of technologies, practices, and controls designed to protect systems, networks, programs, devices, and data from cyber attacks. In the cryptosphere, this means safeguarding the infrastructure of exchanges, wallets, and the users' devices from a myriad of threats.

The permanence of blockchain's ledger is as much its strength as it is a potential vulnerability. Once a transaction is recorded, it can't be altered. Therefore, ensuring that a transaction is authentic before it's added to the block is critical. This authenticity is achieved through consensus mechanisms like Proof of Work (PoW) and Proof of Stake (PoS), which we've explored in previous chapters. Such mechanisms are part of cybersecurity's remit, ensuring that the network collectively defends against fraudulent actions.

Phishing, a type of cyber attack, is particularly pertinent to cryptocurrency users. Attackers masquerade as legitimate entities to steal sensitive data, such as login credentials and private keys. The decentralized nature of cryptocurrencies means that there is no central authority to appeal to in case of theft—hence the incalculable value of preemptive cybersecurity measures.

Social engineering attacks, too, are a pervasive threat, and they often combine the psychological manipulation of people into performing actions or divulging confidential information. This kind of cyber threat exploits human error, often the weakest link in the security chain. Raising awareness and educating users about such risks is as crucial as the technical defences put in place.

Another key aspect is ensuring the integrity of digital wallets. They are the gateways to one's digital assets and can exist in various forms: hardware, software, online, or offline. Each comes with its own set of potential vulnerabilities, from the physical theft of hardware wallets to the hacking of an exchange's online storage. Users must understand the security implications of their choices and the necessary steps to secure their investments adequately.

In addition, two-factor authentication (2FA) has become a standard practice for an added layer of security. It requires not only something the user knows (like a password) but also something the user has (such as a mobile device) to access their funds. It significantly reduces the likelihood of unauthorized access stemming from compromised passwords.

Understanding smart contracts is also vital for grasping the role of cybersecurity. While smart contracts execute automatically based on predefined rules, they're still code and can contain vulnerabilities. Ensuring these are securely written and audited can prevent exploits, which can lead to massive financial losses in the DeFi space, for example.

As for exchanges and trading platforms, they are the bustling marketplaces of the cryptocurrency world and, thus, prime targets for cybercriminals. Maintaining robust security protocols and regularly updating them in the face of evolving threats is a never-ending battle. From Distributed Denial of Service (DDoS) attacks to exchange hacks resulting in millions in lost assets, the cryptocurrency community has witnessed the repercussions of inadequate security practices.

Developing an investor mindset also involves assessing the security posture of the services you choose to use. Just as one would research the stability and regulatory compliance of a financial institution, so too must an investor scrutinize the security measures of the wallets and exchanges they trust with their digital assets.

Lastly, it's essential to consider the most significant asset in cybersecurity: the user. Maintaining a security-focused mindset, practicing safe internet habits, and staying informed about the latest threats and security measures can drastically reduce the likelihood of becoming a victim of cybercrime.

To summarize, the role of encryption and cybersecurity in the world of cryptocurrency is foundational and cannot be overstated. The infrastructure on which digital assets rely demands vigilant, adaptable, and forward-thinking security strategies to deter and respond to cyber threats. Investing in cryptocurrency means investing in the practices and technologies that protect those digital assets—because, in the end, the most valuable currency in the cryptosphere might just be trust.

In reflection, as the cryptosphere continues its meteoric evolution, so too must our dedication to cybersecurity. It's a dynamic challenge, but one that holds the key to a stable and prosperous digital asset economy. Remember, the security you instill in your cryptocurrency endeavors safeguards not just your own assets but also the integrity of the entire blockchain network.

Chapter 9: The Future of Money: Cryptocurrency in Context

As we pivot to exploring the broader horizon that cryptocurrency paints for our financial landscape, the gravity of its impact begins to crescendo. Cryptocurrency hasn't just introduced a new type of asset; it's incrementally redefining what money signifies in a hyper-connected world. With unprecedented speed, societies are beginning to conceptualize a system where currency is not only digital but decentralized, raising profound implications on the fabric of global economies. Navigating this evolution, we delve into the intricate dance between innovation and practicality, shedding light on how traditional payment systems are adapting to the silent beat of blockchain technology. The prospect of a decentralized future fans the flames of transformation, urging us to prepare not just monetarily, but mentally for the paradigm shift that looms. Encapsulating this change, this chapter analyzes how the interplay between cryptocurrency and the global economy could unfurl, and what it means to prepare for a future where financial autonomy could become the norm rather than the exception.

Evolution of Payment Systems

Underpinning the world's economic activities is the complex infrastructure of payment systems, an area that has undergone significant transformation over the centuries. From barter systems, where goods and services were directly exchanged, to the introduction of coins and paper money, society has continually sought more efficient means of exchanging value. But the innovation didn't stop there; the advent of checks, credit cards, and electronic transfers represented the digitization of traditional currency, setting the stage for even more sophisticated systems.

The digital revolution of the late 20th century brought with it online banking and payment services like PayPal, simplifying transactions and reducing the need for physical cash. E-commerce demanded payment solutions that could facilitate fast and secure transactions over the internet, opening up a world of global trade that was previously unimaginable to the average consumer. As technology advanced, so did the expectation for instant gratification, leading to the development of contactless payments and mobile wallets such as Apple Pay and Google Wallet.

While these innovations made transactions more convenient, they still relied on traditional financial institutions and centralized systems. This meant that service providers could impose fees, transactions could be denied, and accounts could be frozen. Additionally, these systems required personal identity verification, leaving the unbanked population at a disadvantage. It became clear that a new paradigm of payment systems could unlock further economic opportunities, particularly those that offered decentralization and financial inclusion.

The concept of cryptocurrencies, first introduced with Bitcoin in 2009, signified a monumental shift in the evolution of payment systems. Built on the blockchain, a decentralized ledger technology, cryptocurrencies presented a way to conduct transactions without the need for a central authority. This promised lower fees, reduced transaction times, and an escape from the constraints of traditional banking infrastructures.

Bitcoin's success led to the emergence of various altcoins, each attempting to build upon or refine the concept of digital currency. Payment systems began to emerge around these currencies, leveraging blockchain's security and transparency. For instance, Ripple sought to expedite and reduce the cost of international transactions, challenging the SWIFT system that banks traditionally used.

However, the adoption of cryptocurrency as a mainstream payment system faced many hurdles, including volatility, legal hurdles, and a lack of understanding among the general public. Despite these challenges, the infrastructure continued to grow, with payment processors like BitPay and Coinbase enabling businesses to accept cryptocurrencies easily.

The innovation in cryptocurrency payment systems pushed the traditional financial sector to explore similar technologies. Central banks started to investigate the possibility of Central Bank Digital Currencies (CBDCs), which could offer some of the benefits of cryptocurrencies, like ease of transfer and security, while maintaining state control and stability.

In parallel, companies traditionally outside the financial sphere started to venture into payments, leveraging their massive user bases and technology infrastructures. For instance, Facebook proposed its digital currency, Libra (later renamed Diem), aiming to provide an accessible financial system for its users worldwide.

With the emergence of smart contracts on platforms like Ethereum, the scope of what could be achieved with payment systems expanded. These self-executing contracts with the terms of the agreement directly written into code could automate and secure complex transactions without intermediaries, opening avenues for decentralized finance (DeFi) systems.

DeFi platforms began to emulate and reinvent traditional financial services like lending, insurance, and asset management, all built upon blockchain's transparent and trustless nature. These systems are not only fueling innovation within the cryptocurrency space but are also beginning to influence the strategies of traditional financial institutions.

As the technological landscape continued to evolve, so too did the threats to payment systems. Thus, the focus on cybersecurity and the demand for robust encryption technologies have never been higher. The ability to secure transactions and protect funds from malicious actors has become a paramount concern for both traditional and crypto-based payment systems.

Looking to the horizon, the fusion of blockchain technology with other cutting-edge technologies such as quantum computing, artificial intelligence (AI), and the Internet of Things (IoT) is likely to catalyze the next leap in the evolution of payment systems. These will potentially provide even faster, more secure, and more intelligent systems capable of autonomous financial interactions between machines.

As the evolution of payment systems continues to unfold, it is bound to shape the very fabric of global commerce. Payment systems are no longer just a means to transfer monetary value; they have become platforms for innovation, enabling new economic models and empowering billions of people by democratizing access to financial resources. The link between financial freedom and economic prosperity is becoming increasingly apparent, and as technology marches forward, the barriers to financial inclusion are gradually being dismantled.

For the reader looking to deepen their understanding of cryptocurrencies and blockchain, the evolution of payment systems is not merely historical context. It is a roadmap to future opportunities, a lens through which to gauge the trajectory of economic empowerment, and a window into the potential for innovation that lies within our increasingly interconnected world. It is this profound shift that we must grasp to responsibly and effectively navigate the vast possibilities of digital currencies and blockchain technology.

Cryptocurrency and the Global Economy

In the landscape of the global economy, cryptocurrency has emerged as a contender to traditional fiat currency, reshaping how we understand money and finance. In this section, we'll delve into how this innovative medium of exchange is influencing the world's economic milieu and its potential ripple effects on markets, governments, and societies at large.

Let's start by examining the concept of cryptocurrencies as decentralized assets. Unlike fiat currency, cryptocurrencies aren't controlled by a central authority. This decentralization has significant implications for economic sovereignty, potentially allowing countries with volatile currencies to find stability in crypto assets. However, this also poses challenges as sovereign currencies could face competition from global cryptocurrencies like Bitcoin or stablecoins pegged to other national currencies or commodities.

The adoption of cryptocurrencies has shown an upward trend, influencing global trade and investment. With cross-border transactions becoming faster and often less expensive thanks to blockchain technology, a seamless international market is within reach. This efficiency could empower businesses – from startups to multinationals – by reducing the friction associated with currency conversion and transfer delays.

That said, the volatility of cryptocurrencies cannot be overlooked. It's well-known that cryptocurrency markets can experience dramatic price swings, leading to both opportunities and risks for investors and the global economy. While this volatility can lead to considerable profits, it can also contribute to financial instability. Investors, especially those new to the space, need to manage risk and approach these markets with a balanced, informed strategy.

Moreover, central banks worldwide have started exploring the concept of Central Bank Digital Currencies (CBDCs), a blockchain-based form of their native fiat currency. The introduction of CBDCs could streamline monetary policies and potentially challenge the existing place of cryptocurrencies by providing a more stable digital alternative with legal tender status.

Remittances, a critical aspect of the economies of many developing countries, are also being transformed by cryptocurrency. With the aim of bypassing high fees and slow processing times of traditional banking systems, cryptocurrencies present an attractive option for migrant workers sending money home. Reducing the cost of remittances could enhance the financial wellbeing of individuals in these economies.

On the flip side of this digital coin, there are concerns about the use of cryptocurrency in illicit activities due to its anonymous nature. The challenge for global economies is to balance the privacy advantages of cryptocurrencies with the need for transparency to prevent money laundering and financing terrorism.

Another crucial aspect of cryptocurrencies in the global economy is their impact on employment and business models. They've given birth to an entire industry, ranging from mining operations to exchanges, wallets, and fintech startups innovating in the space, spurring job creation and potentially altering the landscape of the financial services industry.

Furthermore, cryptocurrency markets are becoming interlinked with traditional financial markets. As a result, cryptocurrencies are increasingly being viewed as a new asset class for diversification. Savvy investors are including them in their portfolios, recognizing the advantages they can offer in terms of high potential returns and as a hedge against inflation.

Additionally, the potential of cryptocurrencies to foster financial inclusion cannot be ignored. With over a billion people worldwide without access to traditional banking services, cryptocurrencies can offer an alternative entry point into the financial system, using nothing more than a mobile phone and internet access.

Nonetheless, the environmental impact of some cryptocurrencies, particularly those that require extensive computational power like Bitcoin, has sparked debate. While many tout the benefits of cryptocurrency, there's growing concern about its energy consumption and environmental footprint, pressing the industry towards more sustainable practices and the exploration of energy-efficient consensus mechanisms.

In light of all these factors, it's imperative for potential investors and participants in the crypto economy to understand the market dynamics. While high returns are possible, the inherent risks associated with such a volatile and relatively new market cannot be practically ignored. Therefore, education becomes crucial, not only in making informed investment decisions but also in understanding the larger economic impacts.

Looking ahead, as cryptocurrencies continue to gain acceptance and regulatory frameworks evolve, their integration into the global economy will likely deepen. This integration, while promising, will require continuous monitoring and adjustment from all stakeholders, including investors, businesses, regulatory bodies, and consumers, to ensure its benefits are maximized and its challenges are responsibly managed.

Ultimately, cryptocurrencies are not just a technological novelty; they are reshaping the way we think about and interact with the global economy. As we move forward, the robust debate and research into the economic implications of this burgeoning asset class will pave the way for its mature integration into our day-to-day financial dealings.

These digital assets offer not only a new investment frontier but also a chance to redefine economic structures for a more connected and efficient future.

To navigate this complex and dynamic terrain, it's valuable for readers like yourself, whether you're a curious individual, an aspiring developer, or an investor with an eye on the future, to continuously educate yourselves. Your quest for knowledge and understanding of cryptocurrency will empower you to participate thoughtfully in a global economy that's being transformed by the blockchain revolution.

Preparing for a Decentralized Future

In considering the swift advancement of cryptocurrencies and blockchain technology, it's imperative to lay the groundwork for a future where decentralized systems are commonplace. As we've learned, the potential for disruption spreads across various sectors, from finance to healthcare. Preparing for this future involves a multifaceted approach, including education, strategic investment, and a strong grasp of technological capabilities and limitations.

Education is, without question, the stepping stone to proficiency. For those aspiring to thrive in the decentralization era, it is essential to obtain a robust understanding of blockchain's foundational concepts. This education extends beyond understanding how a blockchain works or what distinguishes Bitcoin from other altcoins. It digs deeper into the philosophical and economic implications of a decentralized world where intermediaries become obsolete, and trust is established through consensus mechanisms rather than central authorities.

Everyday participants in this new ecosystem must be adept at managing cryptographic keys—the lynchpins of asset control in the crypto realm. Adequate knowledge regarding public and private keys, along with the importance of wallet security, cannot be overstated. As the sector matures, these skills will become as fundamental as using a credit card or online banking in today's world.

Strategic investment, too, is a crucial aspect of riding the cryptocurrency wave. Investors need to comprehend the implications of market volatility and the significance of investment diversification. Embracing a decentralized future necessitates a forward-thinking attitude, with a focus not just on current trends but also on potential future developments that may open new opportunities or pose unique risks.

Understanding technological capabilities and limitations also underpins preparation. Blockchain is not a one-size-fits-all solution; it has both strengths and constraints. Potential innovators and entrepreneurs must evaluate when and how blockchain technology can add value—or when traditional systems may suffice. This discernment is vital for developing feasible and revolutionary applications that leverage the strengths of blockchain without falling into the trap of overestimating its applicability.

Regulations will continue to evolve alongside the technology, and staying informed is imperative. As the decentralized space matures, legal frameworks around the world are likely to change. Engagement with regulatory developments not only minimizes risks but also provides insights into forthcoming changes that might affect the landscape. Whether it's for personal compliance or shaping the regulatory conversation, understanding the legal environment is a key component of preparation.

Security practices are another important preparation aspect. As decentralized networks take center stage, the importance of cybersecurity skyrockets. Individuals and businesses must become proficient at safeguarding digital assets against an increasing variety of threats. This includes encryption knowledge and the ability to recognize and avoid scams, phishing attempts, and other forms of cyber attacks.

Technological proficiency will differentiate the leaders in the decentralized future from the rest. Programming and development skills pertaining to blockchain are becoming as valuable as traditional web and software development skills once were. Acquiring expertise in writing smart contracts, understanding decentralized application (DApp) frameworks, and recognizing the intricacies of various consensus mechanisms will open the door to innovate within this space.

Open-mindedness towards emerging applications of blockchain technology also equips individuals and organizations for what lies ahead. As we've touched on in previous chapters, blockchain's potential extends far beyond digital currencies. Keeping an eye on advancements across sectors ensures that one doesn't miss out on blockchain's transformative applications in industries like supply chain, healthcare, real estate, and more.

Community and network building are also integral. Participating in the cryptocurrency and blockchain communities can provide a wealth of knowledge, support, and collaboration opportunities. Sharing ideas, contributing to open-source projects, and networking can foster a greater understanding and influence in the decentralized world.

On a practical level, those preparing for a decentralized future should begin to incorporate decentralized services and products into their lives where possible. Experimenting with DApps, participating in token economies, and using decentralized exchanges (DEXs) are ways to become comfortable with this nascent ecosystem's dynamics and functionalities.

Professional development should not be neglected. For those looking to forge a career in this space, seeking certifications, attending workshops, and enrolling in blockchain development courses will be vital steps. For investors and entrepreneurs, understanding the market and technology trends will require constant learning and adaptation.

Finally, ethical considerations and social impact have to be part of the conversation. Blockchain technology holds the promise of a more inclusive and transparent economy, but it also raises questions about privacy, security, and equity. As we move towards this future, we must be conscious of the human element and strive to ensure that decentralization benefits all segments of society.

Mental agility will be the hallmark of those who flourish in the decentralized future. The need to adapt, learn, and pivot cannot be underestimated. As we continue to examine the layers of cryptocurrencies and blockchain technology, the preparation for this transformative era moves beyond theory into practical, proactive steps. It's an exciting time to be at the forefront of a movement that may redefine how we conceive of money, governance, and societal structures.

In conclusion, the journey towards a decentralized future is lined with both opportunities and challenges. Though it may seem daunting, the preparation involves an amalgam of education, strategic planning, practical security measures, technological proficiency, and community engagement. By embracing these pillars now, we lay the groundwork for not just surviving but thriving in the new world of decentralized finance and beyond.

Chapter 10: The Tech Behind the Coin: Blockchain Innovators

In the realm of digital currencies, the true mavericks are the visionaries who harness blockchain's potential to push boundaries well beyond the financial sector. These innovators don't merely adapt to change; they're the catalysts, forging new paths and redefining what's possible. Delving into the developers' landscape, we peel back the layers to reveal the ingenious minds and collaborative efforts that propel blockchain from a nascent concept to real-world execution. It's the collective brilliance within open-source arenas that propels the technology forward, where passionate communities aren't just participating — they're leading the charge in blockchain's evolution. We can't help but marvel at the leaps of progress that have transformed nascent ideas into complex, functioning systems — all emerging from the relentless pursuit of innovation in the blockchain space.

The Developers' Landscape

Within the innovative sphere of blockchain, the community of developers represents a foundational pillar. They are the architects and builders, transforming virtual blueprints into concrete digital structures that reshape our notion of currency and transactions. Navigating this terrain requires understanding who these developers are, the tools they wield, and the collaborative and often open-source nature of blockchain innovation.

At the core, a blockchain developer specializes in the design and implementation of architecture and solutions using blockchain technology. They possess a strong understanding of its fundamental operations, such as consensus algorithms that validate transactions, and smart contracts that automate agreements. Learning these skills typically involves a combination of formal education in computer science and self-driven exploration of blockchain-specific knowledge.

Blockchain's attractiveness for developers lies in its potential: it offers a new playground for solving old problems securely and efficiently. Moreover, financial incentives such as Initial Coin Offerings (ICO) and the promise of creating disruptive technologies also lure developers into this field. As a result, the landscape burgeons with both diversity in thought and in practice.

Developers often start by picking up blockchain-related tools and languages, such as Solidity for Ethereum Smart Contracts or learning about the intricacies of Bitcoin's Script. Educational platforms, coding bootcamps, and repositories like GitHub serve as critical resources for both nascent and experienced developers alike. This constant learning curve is steep but rewarding.

An evident trend in the developer's ecosystem is the shift towards decentralized work and community-driven projects. Rather than centralized authorities dictating the development roadmaps, many blockchain initiatives thrive on collaboration and communal decision-making through mechanisms like Decentralized Autonomous Organizations (DAOs).

Scaling the blockchain is another significant focus area, with developers seeking solutions to issues like transaction speed and energy consumption. Innovations like layer two solutions, such as Lightning Network for Bitcoin and rollups for Ethereum, are at the forefront of these enhancements, pushing the boundaries of what blockchain can achieve.

Cryptography also remains a bedrock of blockchain development, ensuring secure and tamper-proof systems. Developers must master cryptographic principles to build trust in the digital assets and transactions occurring on the blockchain. This knowledge is not only technical but also crucial for upholding the privacy and security standards of the entire ecosystem.

While the developer's landscape is replete with opportunities, it also comes with its share of challenges. The evolving regulatory environment, for instance, demands developers to be agile and compliant with varying legislations, which can sometimes hinder innovation or dictate the jurisdiction in which a project can operate.

The open-source nature of many blockchain projects emphasizes communal verification and continuous improvement. It encourages a culture of transparency, peer review, and collective responsibility for the code's quality and robustness, which is a stark contrast to the typically secretive nature of financial technologies in the past.

Tooling also drastically shapes the developer's landscape. Platforms and frameworks, like Truffle for Ethereum development and libraries like bitcoinj for Bitcoin-related applications, provide necessary infrastructures, significantly accelerating blockchain's adoption and application across industries. These tools are continuously refined to keep up with the sector's rapid growth.

Another significant facet of the landscape is the rise in demand for interoperability among different blockchain networks. This has led to a breed of developers focusing on creating ways for distinctive blockchains to communicate and collaborate, further enriching the ecosystem's potential to cater to complex use cases.

Moreover, the push towards mobile and user-friendly interfaces means developers are also investing time in front-end development to ensure their blockchain applications are accessible to the masses. This represents an essential bridge between the complexities of blockchain technology and its practical, everyday use.

Within the blockchain developers' landscape, specializations are emerging. Some focus on the intricacies of tokenomics — designing and managing digital economies — while others hone in on securing smart contracts against vulnerabilities. For every niche, there exists a community and a wealth of knowledge to tap into.

Lastly, the intrinsic motivation and philosophy of many involved in blockchain development cannot be overlooked. A sizable part of the developer community is driven by the potential for societal impact that blockchain represents. Whether it's creating more democratic financial systems or building tools for privacy preservation, the intention to contribute to a greater good is palpable within this landscape.

The developers' era in blockchain is still nascent, yet it is electrified with potential. Every new line of code leads to the possibility of breakthroughs that could redefine how we perceive value, conduct trade, uphold contracts, and maintain privacy. For those who are just commencing this journey or for seasoned developers alike, the landscape is pregnant with opportunity and innovation, making now an exciting time to be at the vanguard of this transformation.

Building on Blockchain: From Concept to Execution

Embarking on the journey of building on blockchain requires a multifaceted approach that combines technical understanding with strategic planning. For individuals with basic knowledge looking to delve deeper into development or entrepreneurship within the blockchain space, the path from concept to execution is intricate but profoundly rewarding. This section aims to elucidate the essential steps and considerations you must undertake to turn your blockchain concept into a reality.

Firstly, defining your vision is paramount. Are you crafting a decentralized application (DApp) to disrupt an industry, or are you looking to launch a new cryptocurrency? Perhaps your goal is to incorporate smart contract functionality to enhance an existing business process. Whatever the case, clarity on the end goal shapes your entire development and execution plan.

Once the concept is clear, begin with extensive research. Blockchain technology is broad, with various platforms such as Ethereum, Binance Smart Chain, or Cardano offering unique features and communities. Understand the strengths and limitations of each platform to ensure its alignment with your project's needs. Engage with existing communities, both virtual and in local meetups, as they can be invaluable resources for learning and feedback.

After selecting an appropriate platform, familiarize yourself with its native programming language. For example, developing smart contracts on Ethereum requires knowledge of Solidity. Aspiring blockchain developers must either possess or cultivate this programming acumen. There are numerous online resources, courses, and forums to help you gain these technical skills.

Designing the architecture of your blockchain project involves blueprinting how the different components—such as nodes, consensus mechanisms, and smart contracts—will interact. It's also crucial to consider the scalability, security, and interoperability of your project, as these factors will significantly impact its success and longevity.

With the foundation laid, prototyping ensues. Begin with a Minimum Viable Product (MVP)—the most basic version of your application that can function. The MVP strategy enables you to test assumptions quickly and iterate based on user feedback before investing significant resources into full-scale development.

Raising funds might be necessary to fuel development, marketing, and operations. In the blockchain world, Initial Coin Offerings (ICOs), Security Token Offerings (STOs), and, more recently, Initial DEX Offerings (IDOs) are popular fundraising methods. However, you must be well-versed in the regulatory landscape to navigate these waters successfully, always ensuring compliance with legal standards.

Engaging with the open-source community can be incredibly beneficial. Many blockchain projects are open source, allowing for community contributions and collaboration. Open source can improve your project's transparency, trustworthiness, and pace of development, given that a vast pool of talent can contribute to its improvement.

User interface (UI) and user experience (UX) design are critical, especially in a field that's notoriously complex for newcomers. Prioritize intuitive design to ensure that interacting with your blockchain application is as user-friendly as possible. This step is often overlooked but can significantly differentiate your project in a crowded market.

Testing is another step that cannot be understated. This encompasses unit testing, integration testing, and smart contract audits by reputable firms. Adequate testing not only ensures smooth operation but also reinforces security, a foremost concern in blockchain development.

Once your blockchain solution is robustly tested, it's time for deployment. This must be handled with care, often involving deployment to a testnet—a blockchain used for testing purposes—before launching on the mainnet, the live blockchain. Monitoring and maintaining the network once it's live is an ongoing process that requires a dedicated technical team.

Marketing your project commences pre-launch but intensifies post-deployment. Given the competitive landscape, clear communication of your project's value proposition is crucial. Utilize social media, content marketing, community engagement, and industry partnerships to build excitement and user adoption.

Continuous improvement and adaptation are part of the journey. The blockchain space evolves rapidly, and staying informed on technological advances and market shifts is vital. Regular updates, community engagement, and responsiveness to feedback will help in refining and enhancing your application or platform.

Finally, considering the broader impact of your project is significant. Blockchain technology holds the potential to transform industries and affect real change in societal structures. Ethical considerations and the overarching mission of your project should guide you, not just short-term profits.

In conclusion, building on blockchain, from concept to execution, is an exhilarating endeavor that demands technical skill, strategic insight, and a responsive approach to an ever-changing landscape. The potential for creativity and innovation is unparalleled, and success is within reach for those who are diligent, patient, and passionate about their vision.

Open-Source Projects and Community Involvement

The world of cryptocurrency is deeply rooted in the principles of open-source software development. In essence, open-source projects are the bedrock upon which cryptocurrencies and blockchain technology are built. These projects are maintained by a collaborative community of developers, with the source code publicly available for anyone to review, modify, and distribute.

Open-source projects facilitate an environment of transparency and trust, essential qualities in the world of blockchain where security and immutability are non-negotiable. Transparency ensures that any stakeholder can scrutinize the underlying code, searching for flaws or suggesting improvements. This collective vigilance helps enhance the security and functionality of cryptocurrencies and, by extension, the entire ecosystem.

The ethos of community involvement is fundamental within the crypto space. Communities aren't just passive onlookers; they're actively engaged participants who propose upgrades, debate changes, and even help in the governance of various projects. This level of engagement is crucial for the evolution and resilience of crypto-currencies, allowing the community to steer the direction of a project and ensure it aligns with the wide array of stakeholder interests.

A notable example of community participation shaping a project is the Bitcoin Improvement Proposal (BIP) process. This procedure allows any member of the Bitcoin community to suggest changes to the protocol. These proposed upgrades and modifications are crucial in maintaining Bitcoin's relevance and efficiency as the cryptocurrency landscape evolves.

Ethereum, another prominent cryptocurrency, has also benefited from a vibrant open-source community. The collective efforts contributed to the development of Ethereum 2.0, which aims for more scalability, sustainability, and security. It's a grand endeavor that wouldn't be possible without a dedicated community of developers and enthusiasts.

The idea of 'forking' is another central concept inherent in open-source projects. In the context of blockchain, a fork happens when a disagreement within the community leads to a split in the project, resulting in two separate paths: one that follows the original protocol and another that diverges with changes. This was famously seen with

Bitcoin and Bitcoin Cash, an event reminding us that the community has the power to influence the very core of a project.

Moreover, open-source projects contribute to a democratized innovation landscape. They lower the barrier of entry for aspiring developers, who can contribute to significant projects, refine their coding skills, and gain recognition within the community. Many developers have started their careers by contributing to open-source cryptocurrency projects, building a reputation that opened doors to numerous opportunities.

Contributing to open-source projects can also lead to financial rewards. Developer bounty programs, sponsored by the project's stakeholders or interested third-parties, compensate programmers for fixing bugs or adding new features. These incentives not only motivate developers but also accelerate the project's development and refinement.

With the proliferation of cryptocurrencies, community initiatives extend beyond coding. Educators, writers, and enthusiasts play pivotal roles in spreading awareness, countering misinformation, and fostering an informed community. Online forums and social media platforms teem with lively discussions, educational content, and support for those navigating the cryptosphere.

Community involvement transcends digital interaction. It manifests in hackathons, conferences, and meetups, all pivotal in forging real-world connections, sparking collaborations, and stimulating innovative ideas. These venues serve not only as a platform for sharing knowledge but also as a crucible for diverse perspectives to challenge each other, fostering a healthy and robust development environment.

Blockchain projects also often employ decentralized governance models, such as Decentralized Autonomous Organizations (DAOs), where token holders can vote on proposals concerning the project's future. Such frameworks empower the community, giving them a direct say in decision-making processes. This continues to solidify the principle that blockchain is not about centralized authority but about the collective input and decision-making abilities of its participants.

One critical function that community members fulfill is the dissemination of knowledge. Their willingness to share expertise ensures that newcomers can quickly get up to speed with the intricacies of cryptocurrency and blockchain. Many open-source projects maintain extensive documentation, tutorials, and forums that serve as starting points for novices to grasp complex technical concepts.

Lastly, the contribution of open-source projects and community involvement expands beyond technical and developmental realms, influencing the very socio-economic structure of Blockchain technology. Community-driven projects like decentralized finance (DeFi) applications challenge traditional financial structures, offering a new paradigm where anyone with internet access can participate in financial systems without the need for intermediaries.

In conclusion, the dynamism and diversity of open-source projects and the involvement of the community are pivotal to the continuous evolution of the cryptocurrency world. They provide the foundational structure for innovation, governance, education, and growth within the ecosystem. As we delve deeper into the multifaceted world of blockchain, it is this spirit of openness and collaborative evolution that will guide us towards a more decentralized and empowering future.

Chapter 11: Alternative Applications of Blockchain Technology

The pulsating innovation of blockchain extends far beyond its debut as the backbone of cryptocurrency; it's a renaissance of decentralized trust. As we dive into the alternative applications of blockchain technology, we unveil an ecosystem where transparency and security become the vanguards of industries like supply chain management, healthcare, and real estate. Imagine products traceable from origin to shelf, medical records at the cusp of immutability, and property transactions with undeniable provenance. These use cases are not the concoctions of an overzealous imagination but the tangible fruits of blockchain's versatility. By tokenizing assets, enforcing smart contracts, and creating decentralized databases, blockchain emerges as the harbinger of unprecedented efficiency and accountability. Its prowess lies not only in disrupting existing frameworks but in forging collaborations that transcend geographical and institutional barriers. Embrace blockchain as it forges uncharted territories, ensuring that as you comprehend its capacity, you're not merely a spectator but a participant in its unfolding legacy.

Beyond Currency: Other Uses of Blockchain

While the financial world has been captivated by the potential of cryptocurrencies to revolutionize money and payments, the underlying technology—blockchain—harbors a multitude of applications far beyond currency. This section delves into the diverse landscape where blockchain technology is innovating and fostering growth in various sectors. As you forge ahead in your understanding of blockchain, know that its capabilities extend into arenas you might never have imagined.

The innovation of blockchain technology is often couched in terms of digital assets and cryptocurrency transactions. However, the application of blockchain extends across various industries, each harnessing the immutable ledger and decentralized nature of blockchain to solve complex problems. Let's explore some of these transformative uses of blockchain technology that redefine their respective domains.

Firstly, blockchain technology plays a critical role in the operation of smart contracts. These are self-executing contracts with the terms of the agreement directly written into lines of code. They facilitate, verify, or enforce the negotiation or performance of a contract autonomously, without the need for intermediaries. This concept can revolutionize various industries, including real estate and law, enabling more secure, efficient, and cheaper processes for transactions and agreements.

One prominent example is in the realm of supply chain management. Blockchain can offer unparalleled traceability and transparency in supply chains—a potent solution to many present-day supply chain woes. By recording every step of the supply chain on a blockchain, consumers can trace the origin and authenticity of the products they purchase. On the industry side, businesses can pinpoint inefficiencies and authenticate the legitimacy of their products, mitigating risks associated with counterfeit goods.

Another area ripe for blockchain innovation is identity verification. With identity theft and fraudulent activities plaguing the digital world, blockchain can offer a reliable solution for secure digital identities. Through blockchain, individuals can have control over their digital identities, choosing when and how personal data is shared online. This not only streamlines online verification processes but also reduces the risk of security breaches.

In the world of intellectual property and digital rights management, blockchain enables artists and creators to have more control over their content. By using blockchain to authenticate and track ownership, creators can ensure they are rightfully compensated for the use of their intellectual property, disrupting traditional content distribution models.

Elections and governance can be transformed through blockchain too. By creating a secure platform for casting and recording votes, blockchain can aid in reducing fraud and ensuring the integrity of electoral processes—a foundational aspect of democratic societies. This could potentially lead to more trust and participation in elections.

Blockchain's impact on healthcare could be profound. Patient data management systems built on blockchain could provide secure, interoperable health records that respect patient privacy while easing data access for healthcare professionals. Such systems would reduce administrative costs and errors, improving patient outcomes through better coordinated care.

Moreover, in the field of academic credentialing, blockchain can facilitate the verification of credentials by storing education and professional certificates on its tamper-proof ledger. Institutions can issue degrees or certificates that can be easily and securely verified by employers, potentially streamlining the hiring process and protecting against diploma fraud.

In the financial industry, blockchain underpins the burgeoning sector of Decentralized Finance, or DeFi. This ecosystem of applications extends blockchain's use beyond traditional banking operations, enabling people to lend, borrow, and invest without the need for central financial intermediaries, potentially democratizing access to financial services worldwide.

Philanthropy and charitable giving can also benefit from blockchain's capabilities. With blockchain, charitable organizations can track donations from the moment they are made to the point they are spent, ensuring transparency and building donor trust. This could lead to an increase in charitable giving and a reduction in misuse of funds.

Outside of these examples, there's a myriad of other potential applications for blockchain. Innovative minds are exploring uses in sectors as varied as entertainment, where blockchain could alter the way we experience and pay for content, to energy, where blockchain might manage the buying and selling of renewable energy credits. The possibilities are expansive and can be leveraged to address specific challenges across different industries.

Of course, these novel applications are not without challenges. The scalability of blockchain systems, interoperability between different blockchain technologies, and regulatory concerns are among the hurdles that must be overcome. However, the relentless march of innovation suggests that such challenges are not insurmountable.

As an aspiring developer, entrepreneur, student, or investor, diving into the world of blockchain applications offers a frontier rife with opportunities. Solutions await those who are prepared to tackle the complexities of blockchain and direct its vast potential towards solving real-world problems.

In conclusion, the blockchain extends well beyond the realm of digital currency. Its promise as a transformative technology has the potential to revolutionize countless aspects of our lives, from how we conduct business to how we protect our personal information. As you continue your journey through the world of cryptocurrencies and blockchain, keep an eye on these blockchain innovations—they may very well shape the future of many industries and, by extension, our daily lives.

Now that we've glimpsed the breadth of blockchain's reach beyond digital currencies, the next sections will dive into specific sectors like supply chain, healthcare, and real estate, focusing on how blockchain is specifically enhancing these areas. Prepare for a deep dive into practical and revolutionary applications of blockchain that are redefining the world as we know it.

Supply Chain Revolution and Blockchain

The integration of blockchain technology into supply chain management heralds a revolutionary step towards transparency, security, and efficiency in an industry that shapes global trade. As we've seen in previous chapters, blockchain's capacity to provide decentralized, immutable ledgers lends itself magnificently to tracking the complex movement of goods and services. Let's explore how the amalgamation of supply chains and blockchain can fundamentally reshape the landscape of trade and logistics.

At its core, a supply chain consists of several intricate processes that include manufacturing, shipping, and retailing. These processes demand meticulous coordination and trust among multiple stakeholders. Blockchain serves as a bridge, connecting these disparate entities through a shared platform, enabling a level of collaboration previously unattainable. This comes as a boon for efficiency and cost-reduction, mitigating the risk of errors, fraud, and delays due to lack of communication.

Blockchain's innate characteristics of immutability and a consensus-driven ledger system ensure that once recorded, a transaction or a piece of information cannot be altered without the consensus of the network. This property is invaluable for supply chain managers who routinely grapple with issues of counterfeit goods, grey market trading, and the challenge of verifying the authenticity of their products.

The role of smart contracts in supply chain management can't be understated. These automated, self-executing contracts with pre-set conditions can trigger actions such as payments or the release of goods, substantially reducing the time and cost associated with traditional intermediaries. Smart contracts, as part of a blockchain system, enhance the enforceability and dependability of agreements across international boundaries—critical for a globalized supply chain.

Moreover, when pondering the potential benefits of blockchain in supply chains, it's essential to consider the profound impact on traceability. Provenance tracking enabled by blockchain allows all participants in the supply chain to ascertain the origin and journey of a product with a high degree of certainty. This is especially significant in industries like food and pharmaceuticals, where provenance can be a matter of public safety.

Inventory management is another critical aspect of supply chains that blockchain technology transforms. Real-time tracking of goods as they move from one node to another can greatly optimize inventories, reducing waste and preventing stockouts or overstock situations. The transition to a blockchain system can lead to significant reductions in the working capital needed to run operations smoothly.

The ability to interlink vast networks of manufacturers, logistics services, and retailers on a blockchain allows for an unprecedented scale of collaboration and data sharing. The resulting network effect not only makes individual players more efficient but also enhances the strength of the supply chain industry as a whole. This potentially leads to more resilient supply chains that can adapt and respond to disruptions effectively.

Blockchain's impact on supply chains is not just about efficiency; it also fosters sustainable practices. With stakeholders having more visibility over their supply chains, they can make more informed decisions about sourcing and environmental impact. Companies can leverage blockchain to prove their commitment to sustainability, increasingly important in a world conscious of climate change and ethical production.

Counterfeit mitigation is another area where blockchain shines within supply chain contexts. Brands across industries lose substantial amounts of money to counterfeit goods. A blockchain's ability to provide a tamper-proof, chronological history of each product also helps brands preserve their reputation and ensure customer trust by guaranteeing the authenticity of their products.

International trade operations see substantial improvements through the use of blockchain to streamline and secure documentation processes, including customs clearances and trade finance. The digitization and decentralization of trade documents take the sting out of one of international trade's most notorious bottlenecks, significantly speeding up global commerce.

With blockchain, the complexity of dealing with multiple parties and jurisdictions in supply chains becomes less daunting. Smart contracts and shared ledgers offer an extraordinary level of transparency and accountability, which is especially crucial when disputes arise. The ease of auditability provided by blockchain can dissuade dishonest practices and promote fairness and compliance.

For the burgeoning "Internet of Things" (IoT) technology, blockchain serves as a backbone that reliably and securely records the vast amounts of data generated by sensors and devices along the supply chain. This synergy of IoT and blockchain fortifies the integrity of data which is crucial for predictive analytics and the anticipation of hurdles within the supply chain.

Despite the numerous benefits, the adoption of blockchain technology in supply chains isn't without its challenges. Concerns over scalability, the costs of transitioning to a new system, and the technical proficiency required cannot be ignored. Training and developing a skilled workforce conversant with this technology are vital steps toward harnessing its full potential.

Amid all these operational transformations, blockchain technology brings a more profound shift—a redefinition of trust in business relationships. The reliance on an immutable ledger over traditional interpersonal trust can reshape partnerships, as reliance shifts from who you trust to what you can verify.

In conclusion, blockchain technology has the capacity to rewrite the playbook for how goods and services move around the world. For businesses willing to invest in this technology and overcome the initial hurdles, the payoff is not just improved profitability, but also a more sustainable, transparent, and trustworthy supply chain. As we proceed through this digital transformation, stakeholders at each link of the supply chain must embrace the potential of blockchain technology to stay competitive in a rapidly evolving market landscape.

Blockchain in Healthcare and Real Estate

The transformative potential of blockchain technology goes far beyond its origins in digital currencies. Two sectors where its impact is particularly promising are healthcare and real estate, each with unique challenges that are ripe for blockchain solutions. As we embark on this journey through blockchain's applications in these industries, we'll unravel how it's not only improving existing processes but also pioneering new possibilities. While healthcare seeks to safeguard sensitive patient data and streamline operations, real estate looks to simplify transactions and enhance trust in property records.

In healthcare, handling patient data with utmost security and confidentiality is a top priority. Blockchain technology, by its nature, provides an immutable ledger, making it an excellent choice for recording medical data. Consider the ease with which medical professionals could access patient histories, knowing that the data has not been tampered with. Such a system would increase the reliability of medical records, potentially saving lives by avoiding misdiagnoses or harmful prescription interactions.

Moreover, the use of blockchain could lead to the creation of a universally accessible and secure database for medical research. Researchers require large data sets to advance medical studies, and blockchain could enable anonymized data to be shared worldwide without compromising individual privacy. This approach could accelerate the discovery of treatments, illustrating blockchain's capacity to serve the greater good.

In the realm of real estate, the introduction of blockchain is reinventing how properties are bought, sold, and recorded. Traditional property transactions are often labor-intensive, slow, and littered with intermediaries, all of which can increase costs and complexity. Blockchain's ledger simplifies the process by providing a transparent and immutable record of ownership and transaction history. This transparency could eliminate fraud, reduce errors, and build trust between parties.

Let's consider tokenization in real estate—converting real property assets into digital tokens on the blockchain. This revolutionizes investment strategies by allowing investors to purchase fractions of properties, enabling more people to participate in the real estate market. It could also facilitate faster transactions and broaden access to international property markets.

Furthermore, blockchain can streamline lease contracts through smart contracts—self-executing contracts that enforce and verify the terms of an agreement digitally. In real estate, smart contracts can automate processes such as rent payments and property management tasks, cutting down on administrative burdens and increasing efficiency.

In healthcare, managing pharmaceutical supply chains is another challenge that blockchain can address. Counterfeit drugs pose a severe risk to patient safety, and blockchain can help ensure the authenticity and traceability of pharmaceuticals from their production to their final delivery at pharmacies and hospitals.

The inherent properties of blockchain, such as decentralization, transparency, and security, align closely with the regulatory requirements in both healthcare and real estate. Regulations demand the secure handling of personal data and clear property ownership records. Utilizing blockchain's ledger, it becomes easier to demonstrate compliance with these regulations, as it provides a clear audit trail.

Blockchain can also enable the secure sharing of healthcare data across institutions and borders. With patient consent, doctors in different countries can access up-to-date medical records quickly, aiding in the coordination of care for tourists or expatriates. This capability is not only convenient; it's potentially life-saving in emergencies when immediate access to medical histories is crucial.

In a sector like real estate, where title disputes are common, blockchain can be an excellent tool for dispute prevention. By maintaining a pristine, easily referenced, and permanent record of property transactions, concerns related to title validity can be significantly reduced, thus fostering a more stable market.

However, challenges to blockchain adoption in these spheres also exist. For healthcare, concerns around confidentiality and data sharing rules can constitute significant hurdles to widespread implementation. Regulatory bodies as well as healthcare providers need to work in tandem to address these issues while preserving safety and privacy standards.

For real estate, widespread adoption requires buy-in from numerous stakeholders, including government entities responsible for land registries. Converting existing records to a blockchain-based system involves a considerable amount of time and effort, and needs to be handled with meticulous attention to detail to avoid errors that could lead to ownership disputes.

Notwithstanding these challenges, we're at the cusp of a paradigm shift. As innovators in both sectors experiment with pilot projects and early-adoption cases, best practices and standards are slowly emerging. These pioneering efforts are laying the foundation for a future where blockchain's role in healthcare and real estate isn't just plausible—it's pivotal.

It's not hard to envisage a future in which blockchain-based systems are the norm in healthcare and real estate. These systems will be more efficient, secure, and inclusive, ultimately contributing to a world where transactions of all kinds are more trustworthy and streamlined. Armed with an understanding of blockchain's potential in these industries, one can start to appreciate the profound changes on the horizon—a future where technology empowers us to solve long-standing problems and create new opportunities. Blockchain is not merely a tool for financial transactions; it's a key to unlocking a future of smarter, safer, and more efficient industries.

Chapter 12: The Next Wave: Trends Shaping the Future of Cryptocurrency

As we've traversed the terrain of cryptocurrency from its inception to its present manifestations, it's clear that the landscape is continually evolving. Looking ahead to the coming wave, several key trends hold the potential to further revolutionize the space. Blockchain technology is poised to give rise to a plethora of innovations with far-reaching implications. Emerging technologies within the cryptosphere are set to disrupt the traditional financial systems as we see the rise of Decentralized Finance, or DeFi, offering autonomous, blockchain-based financial services that promote seamless access without centralized intermediaries. NFTs, or non-fungible tokens, are creating a new frontier for digital ownership and creativity, allowing artists and creators to monetize their work in unprecedented ways. These advancements epitomize the dynamic nature of cryptocurrency, and they're just a glimpse of its boundless potential. As investors, entrepreneurs, or simply curious minds, understanding these trends isn't merely intriguing—it's imperative for anyone looking to navigate the future's digital currents and embrace the transformative power of cryptocurrency.

Emerging Technologies in the Cryptospace

The realm of cryptocurrency and blockchain is continuously evolving, giving birth to a plethora of technologies that could redefine not only how we view money but also how we interact with the digital world.

Let's dive into these nascent technologies that stand at the forefront of the cryptospace, poised to innovate and disrupt in equal measure.

Firstly, it is essential to talk about **Layer 2 Protocols**. These are systems built on top of existing blockchains, like Bitcoin's Lightning Network or Ethereum's Plasma, designed to enhance scalability and speed. Such protocols can facilitate thousands of transactions per second, dwarfing the capabilities of traditional blockchain infrastructure. They represent a critical evolution in the technology, addressing one of the most pressing challenges – the ability to handle a massive user base without compromising on speed and efficiency.

The rise of **Decentralized Autonomous Organizations (DAOs)** is another groundbreaking development. DAOs are entities with no central leadership, governed entirely by smart contracts and organizational rules embedded directly into the blockchain. They offer a blueprint for a new kind of organization that's democratic and operates without hierarchical management.

In addition, we're witnessing the expansion of blockchain use in **cross-border payments**. Projects like Ripple are working to transform the global remittance market, allowing for near-instantaneous and cost-effective international transactions. By disintermediating the process and eliminating traditional bottlenecks, blockchain can significantly reduce the fees and time associated with cross-border money transfers.

Another technological frontier is **Privacy Coins**. Privacy-focused cryptocurrencies like Monero and Zcash offer enhanced anonymity features, addressing concerns about the traceability and transparency of transactions made on public blockchains. They achieve this through advanced cryptographic techniques such as ring signatures and zk-SNARKs, respectively, ensuring the identities of senders and receivers, as well as the value of transactions, remain hidden.

Central Bank Digital Currencies (CBDCs) are a potential game-changer in state-backed finance. Nations are exploring the creation of their own digital currencies, leveraging the benefits of blockchain while maintaining sovereign control over monetary policy. This could streamline economic policy implementation and promote financial inclusion.

Exploration into **Interoperability Protocols** represents a significant stride towards a cohesive blockchain ecosystem. Projects like Polkadot and Cosmos are constructing the frameworks necessary for different blockchains to communicate and transact with one another seamlessly. This is key for the maturation of the industry, as it encourages collaborative innovation and facilitates a multi-chain future.

The concept of **Blockchain Oracles** is also critical in integrating real-world data into blockchains. They serve as bridges between the on-chain and off-chain worlds, enabling smart contracts to execute based on inputs from the external environment. This opens up a world of possibilities for contracts that rely on data such as weather, prices, or other verifiable events.

As for tokenization, **Tokenization of Assets** spells out a future where virtually anything of value can be tokenized and traded on a blockchain. This includes real estate, art, or even shares of a company. This digitization of assets can democratize investing, making it accessible to a broader audience by lowering entry barriers and improving liquidity.

Moreover, the **Quantum-Resistant Encryption** is not just a buzzword. As quantum computing advances, the threat it poses to current encryption standards becomes more real. Blockchain developers are racing to create quantum-resistant encryption methods to secure digital assets against this future computational power.

Focused on sustainability and environmental concerns, **Energy-Efficient Consensus Mechanisms** like Proof of Stake, Delegated Proof of Stake, and others are gaining traction as alternatives to the energy-intensive Proof of Work used by networks like Bitcoin. These mechanisms aim to drastically reduce the energy consumption and carbon footprint of cryptocurrency mining.

On the user experience front, the development of **Simplified Payment Verification (SPV) Wallets** promises a lighter, faster way to transact with cryptocurrencies without having to download the entire blockchain. This advancement is particularly important for mobile applications and users with limited bandwidth or storage capabilities.

Artificial Intelligence (AI) is also making its entry into the space with **AI-Integrated Blockchains**. AI can analyze vast amounts of market data for smarter investment decisions and automate complex strategies within smart contracts, potentially revolutionizing trading and predictive analyses.

Intertwining with the concept of the internet of things, **Blockchain for IoT** is set to secure a myriad of devices connected to the internet. This integration could fortify the security of IoT devices, making them less vulnerable to attacks while enabling transparent, autonomous microtransactions among devices.

The maturation of the space is also leading to the evolution of **Self-Sovereign Identities (SSI)**. These digital identities are controlled and managed by individuals rather than centralized authorities, giving users control over their personal data and privacy. Tied to blockchain, this approach to identity management could revolutionize access to services and online verification processes.

Last but not least, we can't dismiss the potential of **Custom Blockchains and Frameworks**. As the technology becomes more accessible, we are seeing a rise in custom blockchain solutions tailored for specific industries or applications. This trend allows for a more optimized approach to leveraging the benefits of blockchain technology, catering directly to the needs of different sectors.

As we canvass these emerging technologies in the cryptospace, it's clear they carry the potential to reshape our financial and social paradigms. While some will undoubtedly face challenges and skepticism, the most resilient and adaptable among them may just pave the way to an innovative, decentralized future. As investors, developers, and enthusiasts, staying informed and agile in the face of such advancements is imperative. By grasping these technologies, we can better prepare for the novel opportunities they herald and the transformative impact they could hold for tomorrow's world.

DeFi - Decentralized Finance Unleashed

In the flourishing world of cryptocurrency, one term stands out as a beacon of revolutionary promise: DeFi or decentralized finance. DeFi extends the ethos of Bitcoin – the decentralization of currency – and applies it to the broader financial ecosystem. At its core, DeFi aims to recreate and improve upon the traditional financial system by leveraging blockchain technology.

DeFi ushers in a paradigm where financial products are accessible to anyone, anywhere, without the need for intermediaries such as banks or brokers. Instead, smart contracts on blockchain networks like Ethereum automate transactions and enforce agreements. Smart contracts are self-executing contracts where the terms of the agreement are directly written into lines of code.

The DeFi ecosystem includes a wide range of financial services such as borrowing, lending, asset trading, insurance, and more. These services operate on public blockchains, meaning they are open and programmable. This openness fosters innovation, allowing developers to build on existing protocols, enhancing and expanding services quickly and efficiently.

At the heart of DeFi is the notion of 'open finance', promoting transparency and accessibility. Funds are managed by logic written on the blockchain, referred to as 'code is law', which seeks to minimize trust and eliminate the potential for human error or manipulation. As a result, users retain control over their funds at all times, typically via cryptographic wallets, facilitating a trustless environment.

DeFi platforms are often interoperable, setting the stage for a modular financial ecosystem where users can seamlessly move assets and services across different protocols. This interconnectivity can potentially increase financial efficiency and innovation. For example, one can use a decentralized exchange to swap tokens and then utilize those tokens to lend on another platform, all in a matter of minutes and without leaving the blockchain environment.

DeFi's liquidity pools are an innovative solution to a traditionally centralized exchange market. These pools are funded by users' tokens, which are then used to facilitate trades within the platform, and in return, liquidity providers earn fees based on the trading volume. This not only gives users the opportunity to earn passive income but also ensures that there is always a reserve for trading, thus maintaining the liquidity of the assets.

Yield farming, also known as liquidity mining, is another key concept within DeFi. Users stake or lend their crypto assets to receive rewards, often in the form of additional cryptocurrency. Yield farmers actively seek out the highest yields across various DeFi protocols, contributing to the overall liquidity and effectiveness of the DeFi markets.

Borrowing and lending in DeFi are also significantly revolutionized. Users can secure loans instantly without credit checks by collateralizing their digital assets. Conversely, lenders can earn interest by supplying their cryptocurrencies to a liquidity pool, which functions as a decentralized lending platform.

Despite its many advantages, DeFi is not without its risks and challenges. Smart contract vulnerabilities, platform instability, and the volatility of crypto assets can expose users to financial loss. Thus, while DeFi promises to democratize finance, it also necessitates a certain level of technological understanding and risk awareness.

Stablecoins play a critical role in mitigating some of the inherent volatility of cryptocurrencies within DeFi platforms. Pegged to more stable assets like fiat currencies or gold, stablecoins offer a more predictable store of value, which is particularly useful for transactions and financial contracts that require certainty.

The governance of DeFi platforms often incorporates a decentralized autonomous organization (DAO) structure. A DAO utilizes smart contracts for organizational decision-making, eliminating centralized control and allowing token holders to vote on key decisions and changes to the system based on their stake in the network. This aligns with the DeFi principle of creating an egalitarian financial system.

While the traditional finance industry has been characterized by opaque practices and layers of intermediaries, DeFi stands in stark contrast, offering an open-source alternative with unprecedented transparency. Every transaction is recorded on the blockchain and can be audited by anyone, which could, in theory, reduce fraud and corruption.

Amidst its rapid development, DeFi is catching the attention of regulators worldwide. The lack of a central point of control poses new challenges for compliance and the enforcement of regulations. Nonetheless, DeFi communities are actively seeking innovative ways to marry decentralization with regulatory requirements, striving to maintain the integrity of the financial system.

For newcomers venturing into this brave new world of DeFi, a diligent approach to education and risk management is crucial. It's an evolving space with significant potential but equally significant risks. As we forge ahead into this uncharted territory, understanding the nuances and complexities of decentralized finance will be paramount for anyone seeking to participate in this new financial revolution.

The unleashing of DeFi marks the next wave of innovation in the crypto space. As blockchain technology continues to advance, we may see an even broader adoption of DeFi services, potentially reshaping the financial landscape as we know it. For investors, entrepreneurs, and technology enthusiasts, DeFi represents an exciting frontier, rich with opportunities for innovation, as well as a place to be approached with caution and a deep understanding of its intricacies.

NFTs - Morphing Ownership and Creativity

Among the most intriguing developments in the domain of blockchain are Non-Fungible Tokens, more commonly known as NFTs. At the core, NFTs democratize ownership and creativity by enabling true digital ownership of assets. Unlike cryptocurrencies such as Bitcoin or Ethereum, which are fungible and can be exchanged on a one-to-one basis, NFTs are unique. Each token has distinguishing information that makes it distinct and non-interchangeable.

NFTs represent more than just artwork. They can embody music, videos, collectibles, and even virtual real estate in an ever-expanding digital universe. The implications are profound for creators: NFTs offer an unprecedented avenue to monetize digital creations directly, without intermediaries like galleries, publishers, or music labels taking a share of the profits.

The mechanism behind NFTs is underpinned by smart contract technology. These self-executing contracts with the terms of the agreement between buyer and seller directly written into code are the backbone of NFT transactions. They automatically execute actions such as transferring ownership and releasing funds once conditions are met. Smart contracts not only ensure security and transparency but also enable royalty arrangements where creators continue to earn each time the NFT is re-sold.

Understanding the value proposition of NFTs requires a shift in perspective. Traditionally, digital files can be copied indefinitely, which made it challenging to ascribe value to digital art. The blockchain, however, establishes a verified and immutable provenance trail. Owners of NFTs possess something that is verifiably scarce, and thus can be valued much like physical art.

From the perspective of collectors and investors, NFTs represent a new asset class. It's not just about financial speculation; many buyers are driven by the desire to support artists, to be a part of a community, or to gain access to exclusive benefits that NFT ownership can confer, such as invitations to private events or access to additional content.

For entrepreneurs and developers, the NFT space offers boundless opportunities. The technology is a playground for innovation, and new platforms and marketplaces are springing up rapidly. These venues not only facilitate the buying and selling of NFTs but also provide creative ways for interaction and display of digital assets, further enhancing their value.

However, as with any emerging technology, there are challenges and considerations. One of the prominent issues surrounding NFTs is their environmental impact. Most NFTs are built on networks that use energy-intensive proof of work (PoW) consensus mechanisms. Although there is a growing shift towards more energy-efficient systems like proof of stake (PoS), the debate around the ecological footprint of NFTs is ongoing.

Legally, NFTs are navigating uncharted waters. As laws and regulations have not quite caught up with the technology, questions around intellectual property rights and copyright infringement remain complex and are an area of active discussion.

Another challenge facing NFTs is market volatility. Their value can fluctuate wildly, and the nascent market can sometimes be driven by hype and speculation. This makes it vital for investors to conduct thorough research and practice caution, resisting the urge to jump in without analyzing potential risks.

Furthermore, the rise of NFTs has also spurred innovations in how we interact with technology and each other. For instance, virtual worlds, known as metaverses, are gaining traction as venues where NFTs can play a role in shaping identities, possessions, and social status in digital societies. This intersection of virtual experience and ownership illustrates how NFTs are redefining what's possible in the digital realm.

From an economic perspective, NFTs represent a new paradigm in how value is generated and exchanged in the digital economy. They signal a shift away from traditional consumption and toward a model where users contribute to and have a stake in the ecosystems they are part of. Creators can benefit from more equitable economic relationships that empower them rather than the platforms they use.

One cannot discuss NFTs without acknowledging their contribution to community building. Artists and creators are leveraging NFTs to build devoted followings by offering more than just digital assets. They're using NFTs to foster a sense of belonging and participation in projects, creating vibrant communities centred around shared interests and values.

As we delve into the implications and opportunities of NFTs, it's clear that this innovation is more than just a trend. It's a tangible sign of how blockchain technology is restructuring concepts of ownership and creativity, offering a canvas for expression that's virtually limitless. To anyone entering this space, the message is clear: NFTs are not just items to own; they are experiences, communities, and platforms that embody the creative potential of blockchain.

What truly sets NFTs apart is their ability to encapsulate authenticity in the digital world. In an age where trust is paramount, NFTs serve as an anchor point, providing inviolable proof of genuineness. As such, they could be the cornerstone of a new digital renaissance, where creativity and ownership flourish on a foundation built not on scarcity or exclusion, but on verifiable originality and inclusivity.

In conclusion, NFTs are more than a passing craze in the world of digital assets. They represent a fundamental shift in how we perceive and interact with digital content, ownership, and creativity. As you venture into the realm of NFTs, it's important to maintain a balance of curiosity and caution. Stay informed, be discerning, and most importantly, embrace the possibilities that NFTs present for a future where digital realms and physical realities converge in fascinating and transformative ways.

Chapter 13: Embracing the Digital Transformation

The journey through the evolving landscape of cryptocurrencies and blockchain is much like venturing into uncharted waters with the promise of discovering new territories. The shifts in economic paradigms, as unfolded in the preceding chapters, herald the digital transformation that is not only reshaping money but also redefining the very substrate of economic interaction and value exchange. This concluding chapter synthesizes insights from the preceding discourse, offering a reflection on the transformative journey of blockchain technology and its digital assets.

Understanding cryptocurrency goes beyond recognizing it as digital currency; it's about appreciating its potential to democratize finance. Through the cryptographic ingenuity pioneered by Satoshi Nakamoto and advanced by countless innovators, we've seen a financial revolution that has empowered individuals, liberated capital, and spurred a radical rethinking of how we transact. Embracing this digital transformation, as we have discovered, involves understanding not only what cryptocurrency is but also how it equips society with an unprecedented level of financial autonomy and inclusivity.

Now that we've demystified the fundamentals of blockchain technology, let's acknowledge its significance. The blockchain isn't just a technological marvel; it's a new foundation upon which trust can be built without traditional intermediaries. Through consensus mechanisms like Proof of Work and Proof of Stake, we witness the network's ability to align incentives and ensure integrity, which is nothing short of revolutionary. As you continue your exploration of this space, consider how the values transparency, immutability, and decentralization can manifest in various industries beyond finance.

The exploration of Bitcoin and Altcoins has underscored the rich diversity within cryptocurrency. These digital assets demonstrate a collective appetite for innovation and customization that define the ethos of this transformative age. ICOs, tokens, and the advent of new digital assets reflect a market that is still in its youth, brimming with potential for those who dare to invest not just their capital, but their curiosity and passion into this burgeoning ecosystem.

In delving into the strategies for investing in cryptocurrencies, it becomes apparent that while the rewards can be significant, they come with their share of risks. The essence of developing an investor mindset is rooted in the principles of risk management, market analysis, and portfolio diversification. These fundamentals not only protect assets but also provide a broader horizon for viewing investment as a journey through an ever-changing landscape, where adaptability is vital and foresight is invaluable.

Mining has been likened to harvesting digital gold, and rightly so, for it represents the meticulous work required to bring new coins into circulation. Like miners of old who ventured into the unknown to extract precious metals, contemporary miners use advanced hardware in the quest for digital treasure. The analogy symbolizes the sweat equity and technological prowess at the heart of this digital frontier. Moreover, the concept of joining mining pools epitomizes the collaborative spirit defining the crypto community, where success is shared and innovation is communal.

As we have seen, navigating the regulatory landscape is not just about compliance; it's about understanding the dynamic interplay between innovation and regulation. Cryptocurrencies exist in a realm where legal frameworks are still catching up to their rapid evolution.

The roles of KYC, AML, and global regulatory perspectives are not hindrances but guiding principles that can lead to the maturation of the space and a sustainable framework where trust, law, and digital transactions meet.

One cannot overstate the significance of security in the world of cryptocurrencies. Protecting investments extends beyond mere passwords and encryption; it's about developing a security-first mindset. Understanding the digital risks and the mechanisms of defense is crucial in safeguarding investments. In embracing digital transformation, individuals must also embrace the role of vigilant guardians of their digital wealth, because in the end, understanding cybersecurity is understanding the lifeline of digital assets.

Cryptocurrency in the context of the future of money invites imaginative foresight. The evolution of payment systems is occurring in tandem with societal shifts toward greater autonomy and efficiency. As blockchain technology integrates with global economies, the potential for a largely decentralized future takes shape—a future that is inclusive, immediate, and intelligent in its financial interactions.

The technology behind the coin is as important as the currency itself. Blockchain innovators are the architects of this digital era, coding not just lines of software but rewriting the script of economic infrastructure. These developers create more than decentralized applications and platforms; they construct the potential for a world where trust is coded into systems, where intermediaries are redundant, and where the essence of trade and transaction is reshaped for the better.

Blockchain's reach extends, as we have seen, far beyond currency. It revolutionizes supply chains, reinvigorates healthcare record integrity, and provides real estate with unprecedented transparency. Each alternative application opens new vistas of potential, underscoring blockchain's versatility and reinforcing its claim to being the most disruptive technology of our time. Witnessing blockchain's application across various sectors serves as a powerful reminder of its transformative impact and its capacity to rewrite the rules of engagement across all forms of enterprise.

Emerging tech in the crypto space, such as DeFi and NFTs, are not mere trends. They represent the vanguards of a new wave of innovation, redefining ownership, injecting creativity into the digital realm, and unlocking financial services from traditional constraints. These developments are more than futuristic concepts; they are the tangible manifestations of a collective desire to challenge the status quo and champion a more equitable and expressive landscape.

So, as we embrace the digital transformation, let us also embrace a continuous learning mindset. The world of cryptocurrency is volatile, complex, and incredibly fascinating. It promises opportunities for those willing to engage with it mindfully. As you journey through the digital frontiers charted in this book, you are encouraged to probe deeper, learn incessantly, and participate actively. The realization that this is not simply about grasping a new form of money but about participating in the shaping of a new epoch is what defines a true digital pioneer.

In conclusion, cryptocurrency and blockchain are not just technological breakthroughs; they are the dawning of an era where the digital reign is not just possible but imminent. The invitation to join this transformative movement is open to all. It beckons entrepreneurs, students, investors, developers, and visionaries to take part in the crafting of a new digital reality. The digital gold rush of our time isn't a fleeting moment; it's the beginning of a profound shift in how the world views, uses, and benefits from money and technology. It's an era for which we can all prepare, participate, and perhaps prosper. Let's move forward with resilience, ingenuity, and a shared vision for a world transformed by the remarkable interplay of blockchain and cryptocurrency—a world where the digital age is embraced in all its challenges and triumphs.

Chapter 14: Cryptocurrency Glossary

Navigating the world of cryptocurrency can be as exhilarating as it is bewildering, especially for those taking their first steps into this digital frontier. Every field has its jargon, and cryptocurrency is no exception. With its roots in computer science, cryptography, and economics, the vocabulary can quickly become complex. That's why we've compiled a comprehensive glossary aimed at demystifying these terms and helping you gain a deeper understanding of this innovative domain. Armed with this knowledge, you'll be well-prepared to delve into the nuances of blockchain technology and make informed decisions about your digital assets. Here are some essential terms you'll encounter in your cryptocurrency journey.

Address

A unique string of characters that denotes a destination for a cryptocurrency transaction. Consider it similar to an email address, but for digital currency transactions.

Altcoin

Short for 'alternative coin'; any cryptocurrency that isn't Bitcoin. Altcoins can be anything from slight variations of the Bitcoin protocol to entirely new cryptocurrencies with novel features.

Blockchain

The foundational technology behind most cryptocurrencies; a decentralized ledger that records all transactions across a network of computers eliminating the need for a centralized authority.

Consensus Mechanism

A protocol within blockchain technology that ensures all the nodes on the network agree on the validity of transactions. Proof of Work (PoW) and Proof of Stake (PoS) are the most common mechanisms.

Cryptocurrency

A digital or virtual currency that uses cryptography for secure financial transactions, controlled through decentralized networks based on blockchain technology.

Decentralization

The process of distributing and diversifying power away from a central point. Most commonly used to describe the transfer of control and decision-making from a centralized organization, individual, or group to a distributed network.

Encryption

The process of converting information or data into a code, especially to prevent unauthorized access. A fundamental aspect of cryptocurrency security.

Exchange

A platform where you can buy, sell, or trade cryptocurrencies. This can be a centralized service, or distributed, as in the case of decentralized exchanges (DEXs).

Fiat

Traditional paper money, like dollars or euros, that a government has declared to be legal tender. Cryptocurrency is often traded against fiat currencies.

Hash Rate

A measure of the processing power of the network of computers involved in Bitcoin or other cryptocurrency mining. It indicates how many hashes per second the network can perform.

ICO

Initial Coin Offering; a fundraising mechanism where new projects sell their underlying cryptocurrency tokens in exchange for Bitcoin, Ethereum, or other established cryptocurrencies.

Mining

The process by which new cryptocurrency coins are made available and transactions are verified and added to the blockchain, often requiring substantial computational resources.

Node

Any computer connected to the blockchain network is called a node. These nodes support the network through transaction verification and dissemination.

Private Key

A sophisticated form of cryptography that allows a user to access their cryptocurrency holdings. Your private key is crucial; without it, your digital assets are inaccessible.

Public Key

Tied to a private key, this is the wallet address that you share with others to receive cryptocurrency. It can be thought of as your bank account number for the cryptocurrency world.

Satoshi Nakamoto

The pseudonymous person or group of people who developed Bitcoin. The true identity of Satoshi Nakamoto remains unknown.

Smart Contract

Self-executing contracts with the terms of the agreement between buyer and seller directly written into lines of code, and stored and replicated on a blockchain network.

Token

While often used interchangeably with cryptocurrency, a token generally refers to a cryptocurrency that operates on top of another blockchain, such as ERC-20 tokens on the Ethereum network.

Wallet

Digital software that stores private and public keys and interacts with various blockchains to enable users to send and receive digital currency and monitor their balance.

As we pivot towards a decentralized future, these terms and concepts will become increasingly integral to the ways in which we conceive of currency, investment, and even society itself. With this cryptocurrency glossary, you've built a sturdy foundation. Let it be your springboard into the vibrant, ever-evolving tapestry of this dynamic marketplace. Admire your freshly gained knowledge as you stand at the vanguard of the digital age. Welcome to the revolution.

Appendix A: Resource Guide for Further Learning

Embarking on the journey of fully grasping the intricacies of cryptocurrencies and blockchain is like navigating a labyrinth of digital innovation, constantly evolving financial theories, and ever-emerging technological trends. To not just thrive, but excel, in this transformative landscape, continuous learning is quintessential. This resource guide is curated to extend the foundations laid out in this book and empower you with avenues for further exploration, study, and personal growth.

Books and Ebooks

The world of blockchain and cryptocurrency is ever-changing, but there are certain texts that stand the test of time and continue to serve as invaluable resources:

- *Mastering Bitcoin* by Andreas M. Antonopoulos - A comprehensive deep dive into the technical workings of Bitcoin.
- *Blockchain Revolution* by Don Tapscott and Alex Tapscott - Unravel the broader implications of blockchain technology on society and business.
- *Outliers* by Malcolm Gladwell - Although not directly about crypto, this work provides insights into what makes high achievers different, which could be beneficial to your mindset.

Online Courses and Webinars

Expand your understanding through these dynamic learning platforms:

- Coursera offers a range of courses partnered with leading universities, including "Bitcoin and Cryptocurrency Technologies" for a solid groundwork.
- Udemy hosts a variety of industry-specific courses tailored for different levels, providing both technical and trading education.

Podcasts and Videos

Stay updated with real-time insights and discussions:

- The 'Unchained' podcast by Laura Shin offers critical conversations with industry pioneers and is ideal for understanding the evolving market.
- 'The Pomp Podcast' dives into discussions around finance, blockchain and Bitcoin with an engaging approach.
- YouTube channels like 'aantonop' provide comprehensive tutorials on Bitcoin and open blockchains.

Communities and Forums

Engage with like-minded individuals:

- Reddit and particularly forums like r/bitcoin and r/cryptocurrency are teeming with discussions and advice.
- Bitcoin Talk Forum continues to be a goldmine for information sharing and problem-solving.
- Blockchain hubs and coworking spaces often host meetups; find one in your area to network and learn.

Academic Journals and Research

Deepen your understanding by delving into peer-reviewed research:

- The Journal of Cryptology and Ledger, the first peer-reviewed journal dedicated to cryptocurrency and blockchain technologies.

Your mastery in these subjects will not only come from the materials provided but also from your dedication to staying curious, being critical, and persistently seeking knowledge. Let these resources be your stepping stones to innovation and success in the rich, burgeoning world of cryptocurrencies and blockchain.

Appendix B: Investment Tracking and Management Tools

In the journey of cryptocurrency exploration and investment, it's essential to harness the power of tools that provide clarity and control over your digital assets. Robust investment tracking and management tools not only simplify monitoring your portfolio's performance but can also offer deeper insights and aid strategic decision-making. Let's explore how these tools can empower investors navigating the dynamic cryptosphere.

Overview of Tracking and Management Tools

At their core, investment tracking and management tools serve to consolidate your various cryptocurrency holdings, giving you a bird's-eye view of your portfolio. By linking wallets and exchange accounts, these platforms provide real-time data on asset values, transaction history, and overall portfolio growth. They enable you to detect market trends, gauge your investment's health, and make informed decisions based on comprehensive data analytics.

Key Features to Look For

When choosing a tracking tool, there are several critical features you'll want to consider:

- **Compatibility:** Ensure the tool supports all the cryptocurrencies in your portfolio, as well as integration with various exchanges and wallets.

- **Security:** As with all things crypto, security is paramount. Opt for tools that offer strong encryption and protection of your data.
- **Usability:** A user-friendly interface with customizable dashboards and easy navigation will make tracking your investments less daunting.
- **Analytics:** Access to detailed analytics and reporting can reveal patterns and performance metrics that aid in decision-making.
- **Tax Reporting:** Some tools offer features to help calculate capital gains and prepare reports for tax purposes, which can be invaluable.

Popular Tracking and Management Platforms

The market offers a plethora of sophisticated solutions. Here are a few well-regarded platforms:

1. CoinMarketCap and CoinGecko are great for market data and tracking coin performance.
2. Blockfolio and Delta are mobile apps favored for personalized portfolio tracking.
3. CoinTracking and CryptoCompare provide comprehensive analysis tools, including tax reporting functions.

While these platforms have their unique strengths, each also comes with limitations. It's prudent to perform due diligence and perhaps use a combination of tools to cover all bases.

Developing a Management Routine

Consistency in tracking and analysis can enhance the benefits of these tools. Setting aside time weekly to review your portfolio's performance, understanding the impact of recent trades, and keeping an eye on emerging market trends can be enhanced through a disciplined routine. Over time, you'll build a keen sense for market movements that can be pivotal in optimizing your investment strategies.

Moreover, continual learning through these tools can highlight areas where adjustments may be needed, such as rebalancing your portfolio to maintain a desired level of diversification or capitalizing on a shift in market sentiment.

Customizing for Advanced Strategies

As your familiarity with the cryptocurrency market grows, so too can the complexity of your investment strategies. Advanced tools can track not just the valuation of your holdings but also offer insights into the liquidity of markets, slippage, order book depth, and the spread across different exchanges — key metrics for sophisticated trading strategies.

Remember that the choice of tools should evolve with your needs. A keen eye on the capabilities of each platform ensures that your toolset aligns with your advancing investment approach.

Future-Proofing Your Investment Tracking

The cryptocurrency market is ever-evolving, with new coins, technologies, and regulations surfacing constantly. An investment tracking and management tool that stays on the cutting edge, with developers keen to integrate upcoming features and adapt to market changes, is vital for keeping your portfolio future-proof.

Leveraging the right tools and resources can be the difference between navigating the cryptosphere with a clear map or getting lost in its complex depths. As you build your investment tracking routine, think of these tools not as a passive ledger but as a dynamic compass, guiding your decision-making and propelling you toward informed, strategic growth in the cryptocurrency landscape.

www.ingramcontent.com/pod-product-compliance
Lightning Source LLC
LaVergne TN
LVHW100320210926
848480LV00003B/1201
* 9 7 8 1 9 2 3 4 5 2 3 4 3 *